BOOK 2

LEON

Naturally
FAST FOOD

By Henry Dimbleby & John Vincent

conran
OCTOPUS

CONTENTS

John and Henry, December 2009

WELCOME TO
NATURALLY FAST FOOD

When we first started Leon, back in 2004, we tried to imagine what a main-street fast food joint might be like in heaven: a place where fresh, unprocessed, satisfying meals are served with pride. With the help of many people, especially Allegra and Benny, we have made some progress toward our long-term goal of bringing the best food to the most people. In this book, we're hoping to bring some of that heaven home. We want to make it easy for everyone—whatever your level of culinary expertise—to eat well.

We've divided the book into two parts. The first section, Fast Food, is about dishes that can be conjured up in 20 minutes or less, from start to finish. The second section, Slow Fast Food, contains dishes that can be prepared in advance and then quickly reheated when you need them—think of them as your very own ready meals. There are also a lot of bonuses, but we'll let you find those.

This is not a book for the coffee table. It is a book we would like to be used, made messy, torn a little, and stuck together with unidentified sticky stuff.

Henry and John

A note on the authors

We have written this book in the first person plural—"we"—because it is the fruit of our collective loins. It represents everything we—Henry and John, Allegra, and all the other people who have helped build Leon—believe matters most about food.

In reality, of course, we all bring different things to the table. We've shared the writing of the general sections, but when it comes to the recipes, the way it works broadly speaking is this: Henry cooks and John eats.

Henry grew up in a foodie household (his mother is the cookbook writer Josceline Dimbleby), and toyed with the idea of becoming a chef. After university, he did a stint under the great Bruno Loubet, but concluded that he was too messy in the kitchen to make a career of it. Nevertheless, he knows cheffy things—how to chop things so fast you can't see the knife, for instance—and can put together a feast for 20 without breaking a sweat. Food is his first love, and about two-thirds of the recipes in this book are his. But they would not have their distinctively Leon character without …

John—the eater. Although he makes a mean green chicken curry (see page 106), John is humble to the point of false modesty about his own cooking skills. "The first time I offered to cook for my then-girlfriend, Katie," he confesses, "I turned up at her house with a jar of Chicken Tonight." In the years since, Katie has made an honest man of him—and his taste in food has improved greatly. John's interest in nutrition has been crucial in determining the Leon ethos. He believes that there are secrets out there that should not be secrets—such as the glycemic index, the damaging effects of sugar, good and bad fats, and the high incidence of wheat, gluten, and dairy intolerance. John has a good palate and is invaluable at tastings. He is the people's representative at Leon, coming up with ideas for dishes that he thinks people will love, and making sure that the food keeps on tasting good and doing you good.

LOVE YOUR PANTRY

Whether your pantry is a whole room (lucky you) or just a couple of shelves, this is where you'll keep your arsenal of flavors.

These are our weapons of choice.

ANCHOVIES   CAPERS
Nature's flavor enhancers
(see page 128).

TOPPERS
Toasted, to give a little crisp
finish to all kinds of dishes.
NUTS
Sliced almonds, cashews,
hazelnuts, pine nuts.
SEEDS
Flax, sunflower, pumpkin.

HONEY
We use one made
by bees that feed
on orange
blossom
(this makes it
naturally low GI—
see page 294).

SPICES
Even in a small pantry, it's worth going long on
spices. They are the best way to bring a flavor hit
to a quick dish. It is better, if possible, to buy
cumin and coriander as whole seeds and grind
them when you need them, because powders
tend to turn stale relatively quickly.

CARDAMOM PODS[*]
Warm, sweet, aromatic.

**CORIANDER
SEEDS**[*]
Scented
and lemony.

CUMIN[*]
Strong
and
meaty.

TURMERIC
Mild
and warm.

CAYENNE
Hot.

**SWEET
PAPRIKA**
Soft
and smoky.

FENNEL SEEDS
For that aniseed kick.

[*] The curry triumvirate

DIJON MUSTARD

SOY SAUCE

EXTRA VIRGIN OLIVE OIL
Ubiquitous now and rightly so. The healthiest and the tastiest oil. Worth spending some money to get a good one for dressings.

WHITE WINE VINEGAR
Colorless and, therefore, the most versatile of the vinegars.

CHICKEN BOUILLON CUBES

GOOD SEA SALT

BLACK PEPPERCORNS

THE CARBS

SPAGHETTI
The most versatile of the pastas (and if you cook it al dente it's low GI).

WHITE BASMATI
The easiest to cook and most versatile of the rices (lowish GI, too see page 294, but white long-grain rice is okay, too.)

CANS

BARLEY COUSCOUS
The quickest carb of all, wheat-free and tastes every bit as good as the traditional couscous.

NUTMEG
For vegetable purees and anything dairy.

BEANS
For a simple stew, salad, or side. Our favorites are great Northern, but chickpeas, lima beans, green lentils, and cannellini beans all have their fans.

TOMATOES

Other things we keep on hand

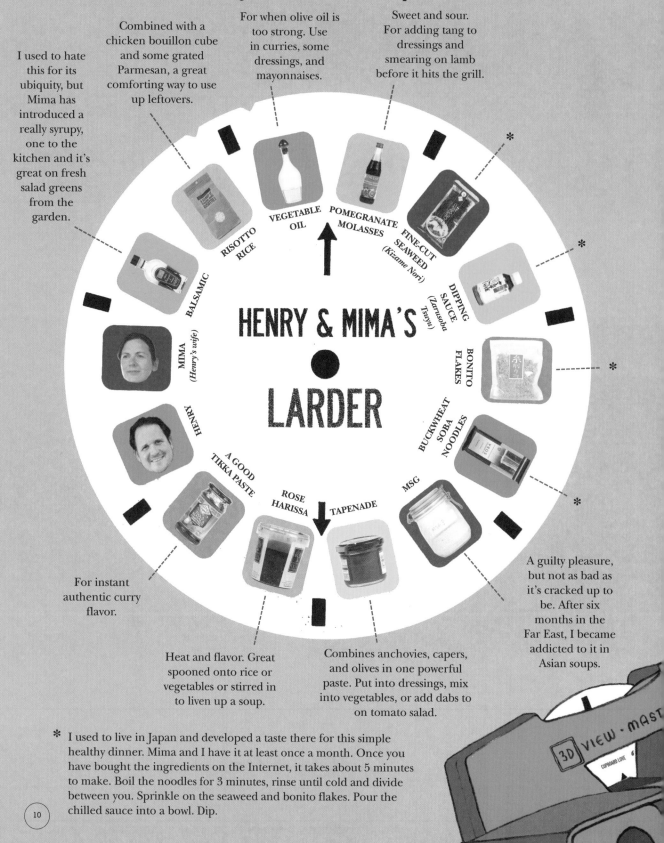

HENRY & MIMA'S LARDER

Combined with a chicken bouillon cube and some grated Parmesan, a great comforting way to use up leftovers.

For when olive oil is too strong. Use in curries, some dressings, and mayonnaises.

Sweet and sour. For adding tang to dressings and smearing on lamb before it hits the grill.

I used to hate this for its ubiquity, but Mima has introduced a really syrupy, one to the kitchen and it's great on fresh salad greens from the garden.

RISOTTO RICE

VEGETABLE OIL

POMEGRANATE MOLASSES

FINE-CUT SEAWEED (Kizame Nori)

DIPPING SAUCE (Zarusoba Tsuyu)

BALSAMIC

MIMA (Henry's wife)

BONITO FLAKES

HENRY

BUCKWHEAT SOBA NOODLES

A GOOD TIKKA PASTE

ROSE HARISSA

TAPENADE

MSG

For instant authentic curry flavor.

Heat and flavor. Great spooned onto rice or vegetables or stirred in to liven up a soup.

Combines anchovies, capers, and olives in one powerful paste. Put into dressings, mix into vegetables, or add dabs to on tomato salad.

A guilty pleasure, but not as bad as it's cracked up to be. After six months in the Far East, I became addicted to it in Asian soups.

* I used to live in Japan and developed a taste there for this simple healthy dinner. Mima and I have it at least once a month. Once you have bought the ingredients on the Internet, it takes about 5 minutes to make. Boil the noodles for 3 minutes, rinse until cold and divide between you. Sprinkle on the seaweed and bonito flakes. Pour the chilled sauce into a bowl. Dip.

3D VIEW·MASTER

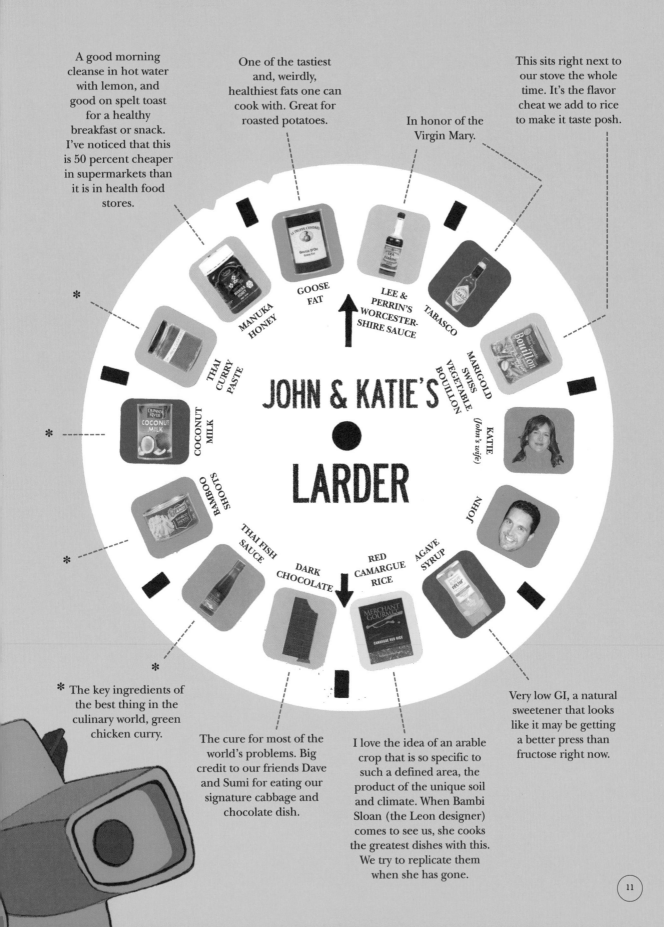

A good morning cleanse in hot water with lemon, and good on spelt toast for a healthy breakfast or snack. I've noticed that this is 50 percent cheaper in supermarkets than it is in health food stores.

One of the tastiest and, weirdly, healthiest fats one can cook with. Great for roasted potatoes.

In honor of the Virgin Mary.

This sits right next to our stove the whole time. It's the flavor cheat we add to rice to make it taste posh.

* The key ingredients of the best thing in the culinary world, green chicken curry.

The cure for most of the world's problems. Big credit to our friends Dave and Sumi for eating our signature cabbage and chocolate dish.

I love the idea of an arable crop that is so specific to such a defined area, the product of the unique soil and climate. When Bambi Sloan (the Leon designer) comes to see us, she cooks the greatest dishes with this. We try to replicate them when she has gone.

Very low GI, a natural sweetener that looks like it may be getting a better press than fructose right now.

JOHN & KATIE'S ● LARDER

MANUKA HONEY
GOOSE FAT
LEE & PERRIN'S WORCESTERSHIRE SAUCE
TABASCO
MARIGOLD SWISS VEGETABLE BOUILLON
KATIE (John's wife)
JOHN
AGAVE SYRUP
RED CAMARGUE RICE
DARK CHOCOLATE
THAI FISH SAUCE
BAMBOO SHOOTS
COCONUT MILK
THAI CURRY PASTE

LOVE YOUR FREEZER

The snobbery once associated with frozen food has disappeared, as people realize that freezing is a great way to preserve the vitamins and minerals in fruit and vegetables. A well-stocked freezer full of things you made earlier—soups, stews, chili con carne, anything that suits reheating—is also a godsend on those nights when you just can't be bothered to cook. It'll stop you resorting to greasy takeouts, and, therefore, make you richer, thinner, and happier.

In an ideal world, we'd all have those vast chest freezers—the kind you can store a corpse in. Instead, most of us make do with something somewhat smaller than the average television. It pays, therefore, to pack it judiciously. If you have a small freezer, don't bother filling it with raw meat or fish. You'll find it much more useful to have pre-cooked food on hand.

Our all-time freezer top ten would be:

(10) Toast (in the form of bread) Sliced bread freezes wonderfully, so you never need run out of a nice piece of grainy toast.

(9) Pie dough Watch a basic casserole become a pie, as your friends look on in awe.

(8) Vodka

(7) Frozen fruit & berries For instant smoothies. Try adding the vodka, too.

(6) A stick of fresh horseradish Peeled and wrapped in plastic wrap. Grate it from frozen and mix with yogurt, mustard, and vinegar for an instant fresh Sunday horseradish sauce.

(5) Homemade chicken stock Best in those little freezer bags because ice-cubes are too small and awkward to handle.

(4) Vanilla ice cream A good store-bought one. (To dress it, see page 194.)

(3) Frozen peas Not just for putting on injuries after football … but because secretly they're everyone's favorite vegetable.

(2) Homemade soups, stews, & leftovers Most of the dishes in the second half of this book are suitable for freezing. Double the quantities and freeze the rest. Freeze food in single portions—you don't want to have to defrost a meat sauce for ten when all you want is a TV dinner for one. (Buy plenty of small, resealable freezer bags, the kind where you can write the dish and date on the front.)

(1) Fish sticks The freezer king. You can buy really good chunky sustainable ones now. Cook from frozen to make the perfect fish sticks in a bun.

GROW YOUR OWN

Painting by Elektra Mandy

GROW YOUR OWN

Mint   Oregano   Thyme   Chives (in season)

Nothing tastes quite as vibrant as food freshly pulled from the soil. And although growing your own vegetables can seem daunting, it really is true that anyone can do it—even if they don't have a square inch of land to call their own.

In this section, we hope to give everyone the confidence to grow something—whether on the windowsill, in the backyard, or in a proper vegetable patch.

WHAT TO GROW *on your windowsill*

Even if the extent of your arable land is the ledge outside your kitchen, you can still be a farmer. Just with a slightly smaller harvest.

It's best to stick to herbs, which are easy to grow, expensive to buy, and don't last long in the refrigerator. The herb flowers also look beautiful in salads.

Getting the right varieties is critical, because many garden centers sell plants that grow well but don't taste great.

Our four favorite window box herbs are:

Mint
Don't take this as a challenge, but it is almost impossible to kill mint. You can buy all kinds of fancy mints, but for our money you can't beat spearmint (*Mentha viridis*), also known as garden mint.

Oregano or marjoram
Greek oregano (*Origanum vulgare hirtum*) has a particularly good flavor and will thrive in a window box.

Thyme
There are some pretty flavorless varieties around, so be choosy. Have a little nibble on a leaf before you buy. Our favorite is the standard garden thyme (*Thymus vulgaris*).

Chives
Slice into salads and sauces for an oniony edge. Try *Allium schoenoprasum*, a specially bred compact species well suited to window boxes.

In addition to these four, sage and rosemary will grow well in pots hanging off your walls. They are both pretty tolerant of drought, so it doesn't matter if you forget to water them, but make sure they are positioned where they won't get waterlogged. We particularly like purple sage (*Salvia officinalis purpurascens*), and you can't go wrong with *Rosmarinus officinalis*.

WHAT TO GROW *in a small space*

Four years ago, Henry had an overwhelming urge to get up in the middle of the night, dig up half of his already small lawn, and create a vegetable patch. These are his thoughts on the experiment.

In the days after I dug up our lawn, in a frenzy of good intentions—and possibly, subconsciously, to placate my wife, who had been fond of the lawn—I devised a detailed plan of crop rotation that would see our miniscule plot provide a third of our fruit and vegetables. And for a while I really tried: fixing nitrogen with beans, liming the suitcase-size cabbage patch, and experimenting with "Three Sisters" planting patterns of corn, beans, and squash.

George in the garden, age 1

It soon became clear, however, that with a patch as tiny as ours, it pays to concentrate on a few winning crops.

These days, I only plant things that:

a) can be grow in sufficient quantities in a small space to be used regularly, and b) taste much better than when you buy them in the stores. It is also fun to add some treats for children. So now we have a less adventurous garden—more Margo and Jerry than Barbara and Tom—but one that brings such a return on the minimal investment I make in it that it is my greatest pleasure.

With the help of my friend and fellow urban gardener Jojo Tulloh (author of *Freshly Picked: Kitchen Garden Cooking in the City*) I have put together a hit list of crops that are reliable, easy, and tasty:

HERBS

Mint, Bay, Marjoram, Rosemary, Thyme, Oregano, Chives, and Chervil	These are all easy to grow. Chervil is beautiful in salads.
Coriander, Basil, Parsley, and Lovage	These are harder to grow. Only for the ambitious.

SUMMER SQUASH

Zucchini 'Soleil F1'	Pick the zucchini before they get too large, checking the plant every few days.
Patty pan 'Sunburst'	Productive and tasty, producing plump shiny yellow patty pan squash.

SALAD GREENS *a huge topic, but here are some good ones:*

Mesclun mixes	Buy a seed mixture if you don't know where to start.
Butterhead Lettuce	You can't go wrong with this.
Arugula	Both wild (smaller spikier leaf) and the more fleshily lobed cultivated version. Great in a salad bowl and peppery on pizzas and pasta.
Sorrel	Is great cut into ribbons for a lemony zing in the salad bowl, or cooked with fish, or in soups, risotto, and dhal. Jojo sees it as a total must, because it goes through the winter shere we live and self-seeds.
Cutting chicory	Also known as Italian dandelion—has a great taste and a lovely undulating shape. It is slightly bitter, in a good way, and very productive.
Chinese mustards, such as mizuna and mibuna	Great for growing in spring or fall, when not too hot or too cold to take you through the winter. They add a hot taste to salad, and work well as a bed for broiled meats (belly pork, chops, etc.); the leaves wilt slightly with the heat, and taste great dressed in the juices of the meat.

STRAWBERRIES

Alpine strawberries	These do well with children, who love to hunt for the tiny low-growing fruits. They like growing in pots, and look beautiful added to a fruit salad or sprinkled over yogurt.

CUCUMBER

Compact bush cultivars	Choose a cultivar for pickling, such as 'Alibi', or cucumbers such as 'Bush Champion'.

TOMATOES

Beefsteaks, such as 'Brandywine'	These are not always reliable, but amazing when they come off, with their soft, fondant, almost seedless interiors.
Plum tomatoes, 'San Marzano'	A lovely flavor and delicately tapered fruits.
Cherry tomatoes (e.g. 'Gardener's Delight' & 'Sungold')	Good and reliable.
'Tiny Tim' and 'Tumbling Tom'	Perfect for hanging baskets, they are pretty and tasty.

WHAT TO GROW *in your backyard or community garden plot*

There are people better qualified than us in the art and science of planting, growing, and harvesting vegetables, and, luckily, they have written some wonderful books. These are some of our favorites:

Katie enjoying the good life

Eleanor seen carrying leeks

Natasha knows her onions

If you are one of the people in these pictures, get in touch and you can eat free in Leon for a year. Photographs by Liam Bailey.

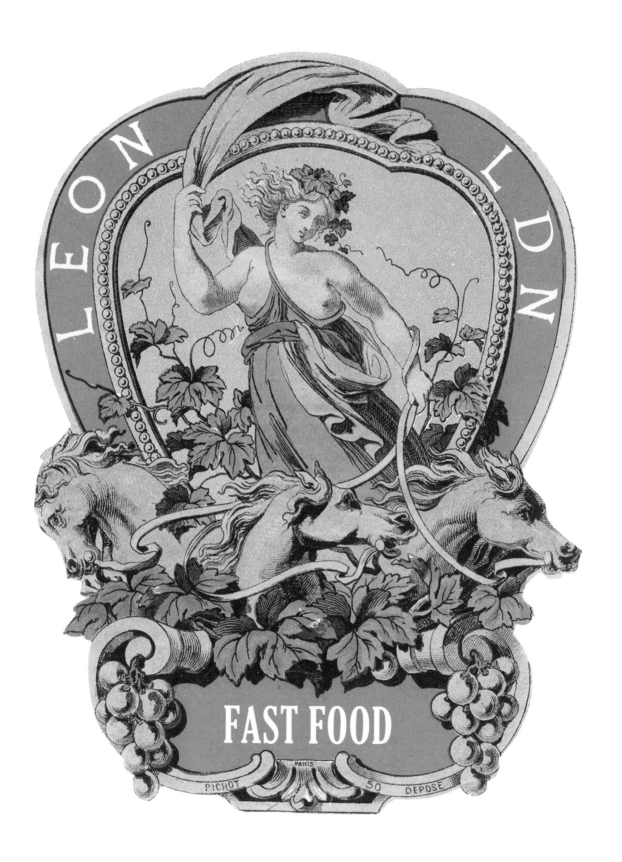

FAST FOOD

This section contains recipes that can be prepared in less than 20 minutes.

A few may require a little cooking time on top of that, but this is time you can use to finish a book, groom the cat, hug your partner, polish your shoes, or catch up on a DVD.

There is a guide at the top of each recipe to tell you exactly how much preparation time and cooking time we think it will take.*

Key to recipe icons (see page 294 for more details)

- ♥ = no or low animal fat
- ✓ = good carbs/good sugars
- WF = wheat free
- DF = dairy free
- GF = gluten free
- V = vegetarian
- (🍴) = indulgence

*We have given times that we think are about right for the average amateur cook.
If you have wicked knife skills, you can probably slice off quite a few minutes.

Fast Food Tips

This book is, of course, one giant volume of fast food tips. But here we thought we'd share some particular techniques for speed and mastery in the kitchen.

SEASONING

This is the most important piece of advice in the book. Even when cooking quickly, take your time to season. Humdrum dishes can be transformed by the judicious application of salt, pepper, olive oil, and lemon juice. Taste carefully. Add salt and pepper. Taste again. If the dish lacks body, add some oil (or a grating of Parmesan). If it lacks taste, a squeeze of lemon works wonders. Squeeze your lemon over a strainer to save having to pick out the pips—a time-consuming and irritating task.

CHOPPING AND PEELING

Speedy chopping—without the visit to the emergency room. The trick is to get the tips of your fingers out of harm's way. Tuck them underneath your knuckles and away from the knife. Use your knuckles to guide the knife. You'll have the confidence to get slicing at speed.

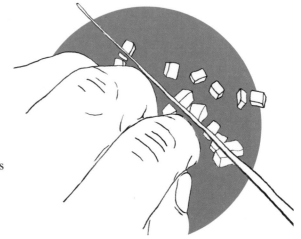

Stay sharp. Pick up a new or second-hand sharpening steel to sharpen your knives, which looks like this (diagram 1), or invest in a fancier contraption, such as a knife sharpener with two rollers and a handle that look like this (diagram 2).

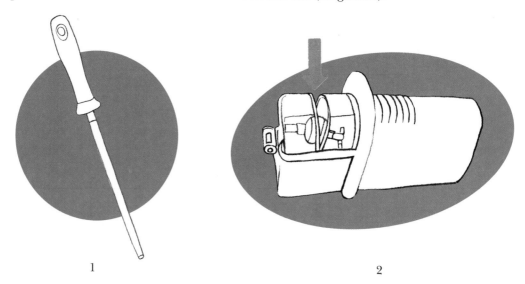

1

2

Invest in a great peeler. Otherwise, the ordeal of scraping away for hours can put you right off your root veg. The best ones are, of course, sharp, with a big gap between the two blades and a head that swivels easily—known as speed peelers.

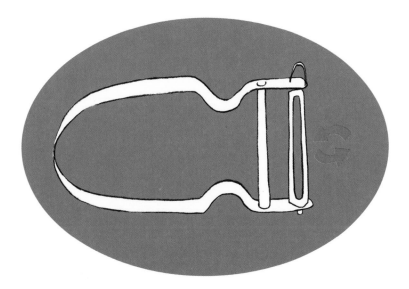

Peel ginger with a teaspoon. It saves time and waste.

COOKING

Minimize kitchen miles. So much time can be wasted walking back and forth when making food. Don't keep walking over to the trash: make a pile of waste. Keep the pans near the stove, and ideally design your kitchen with the sink, refrigerator, and oven arranged in a triangle so that nothing is ever too far from reach.

Listen to music. Pop on your iPod and rev up the tempo. We don't actually know scientifically whether this makes you go faster, but it feels like it.

PREPARATION

Keep a good stock of Parmesan, onions, and garlic. Almost any other ingredients can be made appetizing with these three must-keep-teers. (You can add lemons, too, if you miss d'Artagnan.)

Organize your cupboards and cabinets. When you're in a hurry, it can be infuriating trying to locate the measuring cup or slotted spoon. So make sure everything has its place, as Grandma Edith used to say.

Take this book to work. You can read it on the way in, or on the way home. Or maybe at lunchtime. Or instead of looking at Facebook. That way you'll be able to start cooking the moment you get in.

RAPID BREAKFASTS

For Kurt Vonnegut, "the breakfast of champions" was a martini. For Robert Burns it had to be oatmeal. According to Truman Capote, Marilyn Monroe knew how to eat it with gusto, while Audrey Hepburn did not.

BREAKFAST IS THE MOST IMPORTANT MEAL OF THE DAY

eggy
soldiers

We are creatures of habit in the morning, but what all nutritional experts agree is that:

BREAKFAST IS THE MOST IMPORTANT MEAL OF THE DAY

It is also eaten when we are not at our most inspired and we don't have much time. So, here are a few ideas that might help you break out of a breakfast rut.

OMELETS

For quick eggy breakfasts, omelets are the way to go. Great scrambled eggs take too long, and poached eggs need company (see The Full Works, page 32). An omelet, on the other hand, can be a full meal on a plate in under 5 minutes.

OMELET BAVEUSE: *The world's greatest omelet*

Discovering an omelet "baveuse" is a game-changing moment in life. We were taught how to make them by our French friend Pierre. Many people leave the center of the omelet a little moist or tacky like this, but there is a particular quality that can only come from cooking them at a low heat.

Pierre, Brighton 1976

FRIENDS & FAMILY RECIPES

Preparation time: 2 minutes
Cooking time: 2–3 minutes
✓ WF GF V

2 **eggs** per person
1 tablespoon grated **cheddar cheese** per person
1 heaping spoonful of **crème fraîche** per person
a dash of **vegetable oil**
sea salt and **freshly ground black pepper**

1. Put the eggs, cheese, seasoning, and crème fraîche into a bowl. Whip them up a little with a fork so that they are well mixed.

2. Get a nonstick skillet reasonably hot and heat a dash of vegetable oil.

3. Pour in the egg mixture and tilt the skillet so that it spreads around the bottom. With a wooden spatula, circle the edge of the skillet and make sure that the edges remain loose. After 15 seconds reduce the heat to low.

4. When the top has a moist, tacky texture (see the photo), use the spatula to fold one side of the omelet over onto itself and slide it onto a plate. The omelet should be just colored on the underside, and still slightly runny inside.

5. Eat immediately.

 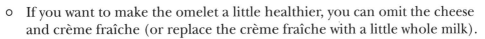

TIPS

o If you want to make the omelet a little healthier, you can omit the cheese and crème fraîche (or replace the crème fraîche with a little whole milk).

o Great for a quick lunch or light dinner, served with crusty bread and lettuce salad.

The fillings Thirty seconds into cooking you can add a filling. We particularly like:

Healthy: Tomato and turmeric. Heat a little oil in a very hot pan. Coarsely chop a tomato (1 per person) and add it to the smoking oil. Toss vigorously—some of the oil may flare up, so don't do this in flammable pajamas. Add a generous pinch of turmeric and season well. The tomatoes should still have shape but will be a bit saucy.

Classic & classy: Add fromage blanc or cream cheese, smoked salmon, and chives.

Cheesy: Add ½ cup more grated cheese per person, with chopped chives and parsley.

Mushroomy: Put Ultimate Mushrooms on Toast (page 110) inside the omelet instead.

Hammy: Prosciutto, crispy bacon, or any other finely chopped cured meat.

THE FULL WORKS *with easy poached eggs*

Like many good things in life, this is all about timing. Not a manic 3-Michelin-starred timing, but the right thing under the broiler at the right time—so that you have time to make sure the coffee is just so.

Feeds: 2
Preparation time: 0 minutes
Cooking time: 20 minutes
✓ DF

2 **tomatoes**
2 large or 4 small flat portobello **mushrooms**
olive oil
2 free-range **eggs**
4 slices of your favorite **bacon**
2 fat or 4 thin link or patty **pork sausages**
1 slice of **bread** per person—optional
sea salt and **freshly ground black pepper**

Minutes

1. Turn your broiler on fairly high. Tear off a sheet of aliminum foil and put it shiny side down on a wide baking sheet. — **0:00**

2. Cut your tomatoes and put them at one end in a row, followed by a neat row of whole mushrooms. Drizzle with a little olive oil and season well. Place the sausages on the baking sheet as well. Put the baking sheet under the broiler—on the highest shelf. — **0:01**

3. Set up 2 teacups and tear off a piece of plastic wrap for each one. Line the teacups and crack an egg into each. (If you are a confident egg poacher with superfresh eggs, just do it your normal way at the end.) — **0:03**

4. Put the bacon on the broiler pan and return it to the broiler. — **0:06**

    Fill a small saucepan two-thirds full with water, and put the pan on the stove to boil.

    Bring up the edges of the plastic wrap to a tight twist, leaving a little airspace next to the egg.

5. Turn the sausages and bacon and put back under the broiler for another 5 minutes. — **0:11**

6. If you like to have toast, get your bread either in the toaster. — **0:12**

    Gently drop your egg packages into the boiling water in the pan, turn the heat down to a simmer, and set your timer for 4 minutes for soft eggs or 5 for hard.

7. Assemble your breakfast on 2 plates. The eggs will be fine out of the water, in their plastic wrap, for a minute or two. — **0:16**

TIPS

○ Depending on the quality (and size) of your bacon and sausages, the time under the broiler will wax or wane to get perfect crispy bacon or the best browned sausages.

WONDERFUL YOGURT

YOGURT *with rose petal jam*

WF GF V

Fill a bowl with rich plain yogurt and cover liberally with rose petal jam (available from Middle Eastern stores).

SWISS-STYLE MUESLI

Makes: 2 cups
Preparation time: 12 hours
Cooking time: 0 minutes
♥ ✓ WF GF V

1⅓ cups **rolled oats**
1⅓ cups **apple juice**

1. In a large bowl, or airtight plastic container, mix the oats with the apple juice, cover, and refrigerate overnight.

TIPS

○ Add flaxseeds or any other seeds you may desire. Soaking flaxseeds overnight helps them to release the Omega-3s.

○ Fantastic eaten with plain yogurt and plenty of chopped fruit.

Tastes Good
Does You Good

MINI KNICKERBOCKER GLORY

Makes: 2 glasses
Preparation time: 5 minutes
Cooking time: 0 minutes

♥ ✓ V

1 small **mango**
1¼ cups **natural yogurt**
1–2 tablespoons **blackberry compote** (see page 260)
  or **preserves**
1 tablespoon **honey**
⅔ cups **granola**

1. Peel and chop the mango into little cubes.

2. Take 2 clean, medium glasses and spoon a layer of yogurt into the bottom of each one.

2. Top this with compote, followed by honey, and a further layer of yogurt.

3. Sprinkle some chopped mango over the yogurt, and finally top each glass with the granola.

TIPS

○ If you do not have compote or preserves, use fresh berries.

A BREAKFASTY BANANA SPLIT

Feeds: 2
Preparation time: 5 minutes
Cooking time: 5 minutes

WF GF V

2 **bananas**
1 **apple**
⅛ cup **nuts**—cashews, hazelnuts, macadamias
1 tablespoon **butter**
2 tablespoons **plain yogurt**
1 tablespoon **honey**
2 tablespoons **Swiss-Style Muesli** (see page 35)

1. Peel the bananas and cut them in half lengthwise.

2. Core and coarsely chop up the apple. Toast the nuts over medium heat in a dry skillet, then remove and coarsely chop.

2. Heat the butter in a heavy skillet, add the honey, and cook the bananas flat side down for 3 minutes, or until golden.

3. In a clean bowl, mix together the yogurt, the muesli, the chopped apple, and the toasted nuts.

4. Place the bananas on your breakfast plate (2 halves each), and top with the yogurt and nut mixture.

Above: Mini Knickerbocker Glory

Below: A Breakfasty Banana Split

What's a kale like you doing on a nice page like this?

QUICK SMOOTHIES & JUICES

The breakfast power smoothie has been a fixture on the Leon menu since we first opened on Carnaby Street. Like the sorcerer's apprentice, however, we are unable to resist the temptation to tinker. Here are some of our most successful experiments.

STRAWBERRY POWER SMOOTHIE

When we introduced this to our menu, one of our regulars described it as "another small step for mankind."

Makes: 2 medium glasses
Preparation time: 5 minutes
Cooking time: 0 minutes
✓ WF GF V

1 small **banana**
a small handful of fresh or frozen **strawberries**
⅔ cup **rolled oats**
1 tablespoon **clear honey**
½ cup **Greek yogurt**
⅔ cup **whole milk**

1. Peel the banana, and hull the strawberries.

2. Put all the ingredients into a smoothie machine or a blender and process together.

 TIPS

o If you can't get your hands on fresh or frozen strawberries, you can add strawberry preserves.

BLACKBERRY POWER SMOOTHIE

We put this onto the menu in fall, when it's getting a little late for strawberries.

Makes: 2 medium glasses
Preparation time: 5 minutes
Cooking time: 0 minutes
✓ WF GF V

1 small **banana**
a small handful of fresh or frozen **blackberries**
⅔ cup **rolled oats**
1 tablespoon **honey**
½ cup **Greek yogurt**
⅔ cup **whole milk**

1. Peel the banana, and pick over the blackberries.

2. Put all the ingredients into a smoothie machine or a food processor and process them together.

 TIPS

o If you can't get your hands on fresh or frozen blackberries, you can add blackberry preserves.

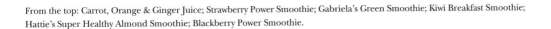

From the top: Carrot, Orange & Ginger Juice; Strawberry Power Smoothie; Gabriela's Green Smoothie; Kiwi Breakfast Smoothie; Hattie's Super Healthy Almond Smoothie; Blackberry Power Smoothie.

KIWI BREAKFAST SMOOTHIE

For those who don't like bananas, this smoothie makes a great substitute.

Makes: 4 medium glasses
Preparation time: 5 minutes
Cooking time: 0 minutes
♥ ✓ WF GF V

2 **kiwis**
a large handful of **berries** of your choice
1 teaspoon **flaxseeds**
1 teaspoon **sunflower seeds**
½ cup **Greek yogurt**
½ cup **fresh orange juice**

1. Peel the kiwis and wash the berries.

2. Put all the ingredients into a smoothie machine or a blender and process together until smooth.

HATTIE'S SUPERHEALTHY ALMOND SMOOTHIE

And for those who are looking for something dairy free . . .

Makes: 2 medium glasses
Preparation time: 5 minutes
Cooking time: 0 minutes
♥ WF DF GF V

1 **kiwi**
1 medium **banana**
2 large handfuls of **berries**—whatever is in season
8 **almonds**, skins on
2 heaping tablespoons **rolled oats**
1 tablespoon **pumpkin seeds**
1 tablespoon **sunflower seeds**
1 cup **rice milk**, **almond milk**, or **soy milk**

1. Peel the kiwis and the banana. Wash the berries.

2. Put all the ingredients into a smoothie machine or a blender and process together until smooth.

Hattie, summer 2009

FRIENDS & FAMILY RECIPES

CARROT, ORANGE & GINGER JUICE

A great cold-buster, this has become a regular on the Leon menu.

Makes: 2 medium glasses
Preparation time: 5 minutes
Cooking time: 0 minutes
♥ ✓ WF DF GF V

3 **carrots**
a thumb-size piece of **fresh ginger**
2 cups freshly squeezed **orange juice**

1. Peel the carrots and the ginger.

2. Juice both in a juicing machine and pour into a large pitcher.

3. Add the freshly squeezed orange juice and mix well.

o   If you only have a carton of orange juice, this is a great way to pep it up.

GABRIELA'S GREEN SMOOTHIE

Gabriela is a friend of ours who specializes in raw food (see page 152). This is not one for the fainthearted. Some of us love it, for others it is inedible. It is made possible by the fact that raw kale is surprisingly sweet—try biting off a piece.

Makes: 6 glasses
Preparation time: 5 minutes
Cooking time: 0 minutes
♥ ✓ WF GF V

4 **kale** leaves, stems removed
1 cup **milk** or a dairy-free alternative,
    e.g. **rice milk, soy milk,** or **nut milk**
1 **banana**
1 **pear**
1 tablespoon **honey**
1 tablespoon **almond butter**
1 level tablespoon **unsweetened cocoa
    powder** (or, for raw food fanatics,
cacao powder)

Gabriela preparing a
feast, December 2009

1. Start by blending the kale with the milk and ⅔ cup of water until there are no more chunks.

2. Add the rest of the ingredients and blend well.

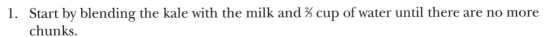

o   If you can't find almond butter, use peanut butter.

FRIENDS & FAMILY
RECIPES

OATMEAL

Oatmeal, aka, porridge is enjoying something of a comeback after years in the wilderness. Not only is it low GI, which means it keeps you feeling full for longer; it also magically lowers cholesterol levels. And best of all, it's a perfect vehicle for all kinds of scrumptious toppings. We serve bucketfuls of the stuff at Leon every day and are registered addicts.

BASIC PORRIDGE

To make oatmeal quickly, use rolled oats—not the steel-cut ones, which take ages to cook. In the restaurants we make it with whole organic milk. At home, we often make it with water—it depends how creamy you are feeling.

(Oats are gluten free, but have often been milled in a mill that also processes wheat. Be sure to check if this is important to you.)

Feeds: 2
Preparation time: 0 minutes
Cooking time: 5 minutes

♥ ✓ WF DF GF V

1 cup **rolled oats**
2 cups **water** (or **milk**, or a combination of the two)
salt

1. Put the oats, water, and a good pinch of salt into a saucepan and cook over medium heat for 4–5 minutes, stirring occasionally.

2. Serve.

Classic oatmeal toppers

○ Cold milk with honey, a blob of jam, some dark brown sugar, or maple syrup.

○ As above, but with heavy cream (Sundays only).

○ Banana slices and honey (see opposite).

○ Crispy bacon and maple syrup (a favorite with Daddy Bear—see opposite).

○ Fruity feast—an extravaganza of fresh fruit, compote, toasted nuts and seeds, and honey.

Leon originals—favorites from the restaurants

○ Valrhona chocolate flakes

○ Banana, orange blossom honey, and toasted seeds

○ Blackberry or strawberry compote

Opposite: Oatmeal topped with crispy bacon and maple syrup, a fruity feast, and banana slices and honey

When we were kids, we would stay in Scotland for New Year. Every morning, oatmeal would be served from a huge bowl. Any leftovers would be poured into one of two "oatmeal drawers" and left to set. The previous day's drawer would then be turned out and the porridge—all shiny and set—cut into bars for a long prelunch walk. They were surprisingly good.
Henry

TOPPED RYE BREAD

Of all the quick breakfasts, these are the quickest. Rye bread freezes well and toasts directly from frozen. It is wheat, and often yeast, free.

Most importantly, the modern rye breads no longer taste of Ukrainian footwear. They are soft and sweet and remarkably addictive.

What follows are ideas instead of recipes—we hope they will spark you into making some rye creations of your own.

New York Breakfast WF
The classic rye breakfast. Toast the rye. Smear on cream cheese. Top with smoked salmon, cucumber slices, chopped ripe tomatoes, and finely sliced red onion. Squeeze with some lemon juice and sprinkle with chopped chives.

Cream Cheese & Blueberry Preserves WF V
Think yogurt and preserves, but on an open sandwich.

Peanut Butter & White Grapes ♥ WF DF V
This is the healthy version of peanut butter and jelly. Slice the grapes in half and either plonk them loosely on the peanut butter or arrange them in military rows for that classic '70s look.

Other rye toppers we love

The European	Like the New York breakfast, but substitute a good ham for the smoked salmon.
The Fruit & Nut	Any other combination of fruit and peanut butter. Fine slices of apple are particularly good.
Hot Berries	Heat honey, ground cinnamon, and berries in a saucepan until the berries begin to lose their edges. Put onto the rye and top with a blob of yogurt.
The Wimbledon	Strawberries and banana tossed in a little thick yogurt, with a touch of honey drizzled on top.
Honey & Banana Slices	Spread the honey on the rye and arrange the banana slices geometrically, just because it looks pretty.
The Full English	Sliced tomatoes (on the bottom), scrambled egg, and a crispy slice of bacon.
The Veggie English	Sliced tomatoes, topped with mushrooms that have been quick-fried in superhot olive oil.
The Reichstag	Whole-grain mustard on the bottom, then sliced tomatoes, ham, and finely sliced dill pickles. For extremists only.

From the top: New York Breakfast; Peanut Butter & White Grapes; Cream Cheese & Blueberry Preserves

SATURDAY PANCAKES

For a luxurious—but wheat-free—start to Saturday morning.

Feeds: 4
Preparation time: 15 minutes
Cooking time: 15 minutes
♥ WF

3 **eggs**
1 cup **buckwheat flour**
1 large teaspoon **honey**
a big pinch of **baking powder**
generous ½ cup **organic milk**
sea salt

1. Separate the eggs. Place the yolks in a large bowl and add the buckwheat flour.

2. Add the honey, baking powder, and a pinch of salt and mix thoroughly. Slowly add the milk to make a smooth batter. You can do all this the night before.

3. In a separate bowl, whisk the egg whites to firm peaks and fold gently into the yolk mixture.

4. Heat a nonstick skillet, gently drop in spoonfuls of the batter, and cook for 2–3 minutes on each side.

 TIPS

You can devise all kinds of toppings for your pancakes, but here are three of our favorites:

○ **Luxury:** caramelized apple and cream. Foam a pat of butter in a skillet, toss in diced apples (1 apple per person), a sprinkling of cinnamon, and a little sugar, and sauté until brown. Remove from the heat and stir in some heavy cream at the end.

○ **Fruity:** blueberries, sliced banana, and agave syrup.

○ **John's chocolate pancakes:** John will eat chocolate with almost anything. This makes a surprisingly good breakfast. Banana, grated, semisweet dark chocolate (70 percent cocoa solids), and agave syrup.

Saturday Pancakes with Caramelized Apple and Cream

QUICK DINNERS & LUNCHES

VEG DISHES *Principles*

We have put our vegetable recipes near the front of the book because, increasingly, we regard veg as the main event of a good lunch or dinner. There are a lot of reasons why: they are good for us; they put less pressure on the increasingly stressed stock of farming land; and, of course, our moms told us to. But the best reason to eat your veg is that, done right, they can be so darn tasty.

Instead of making meat or fish the centerpiece of a feast, try serving three or four vibrant vegetable dishes with a small amount of flesh on the side—almost like a garnish.

Here are some general tips for making the most of your veg.

Tips for creating great vegetable dishes

Think color: People start eating with their eyes, so think about how you can combine vegetables of different colors in one dish. In these pages, you will find vibrant chile on broccoli; the warm orange and reds of carrot and beet; green beans banded with sweet red tomatoes and golden garlic.

Think architecture: Shape and texture are critical to the way you taste. Stay that hand before it slices another carrot circle! Try cutting them diagonally, in batons, into rough, random shapes. Think about how the vegetables will look together and how they will feel in the mouth.

Think texture: There is a received wisdom currently—in our view misplaced—that one should cook all vegetables so they still have an audible crunch. Broccoli, green beans, and carrots will all absorb dressings and other flavors better if they are a little softer. Ripped vegetables have their place, but there is room for soft curves as well.

Think toppers: Something a little crispy on top makes vegetables a bit special. We like toasted nuts (slivered almonds, pine nuts, cashews, smashed hazelnuts), golden crisped garlic, crispy shallots, pan-toasted bread crumbs, toasted seeds, and Parmesan crusts.

Think flavor enhancers: Not MSG but the natural ones—olives, chiles, capers, anchovies, soy sauce, harissa. Don't be scared to give your vegetables a big flavor kick.

NATURAL FAST FOOD

Clockwise from the top: Roasted Crispy
Cauliflower with Turmeric; Carrots & Beets
with Toasted Almonds; Purple Baby Broccoli
with Beans & Hazelnuts

ROASTED CRISPY CAULIFLOWER *with turmeric*

Simple and delicious—great with beer or as a side.

Feeds: 4
Preparation time: 3 minutes
Cooking time: 30 minutes
♥ ✓ WF DF GF V

1 **cauliflower**
¼ cup **extra virgin olive oil**
1 teaspoon **turmeric**
1 teaspoon **black onion seeds**
sea salt and **freshly ground black pepper**

This is a dish that my mom always used to make and has become a popular hand-me-down in our family. Wonderful as a snack before dinner or with a couple of other vegetable dishes as an evening meal.
Henry

1. Preheat the oven to 400°F.

2. Cut the cauliflower into thumb-size florets, discarding the stem, and put into a roasting pan. Add the oil, turmeric, onion seeds, salt, and pepper and toss. Spread out evenly in the pan.

3. Put into the oven for 30 minutes, shuffling the pan once after 15 minutes.

 TIPS

o You can use a curry or tikka paste from a jar instead of turmeric.

o The smaller florets can get a bit burned, but that can be nice.

o Good with feta crumbled over the top and served with a salad for a simple dinner.

o Fred loves it with yogurt, mixed with chile and lime juice.

CARROTS & BEETS *with slivered almonds*

Beautiful to look at and extremely straightforward to make (pictured on page 51).

Feeds: 4 (with room to spare)
Preparation time: 5 minutes
Cooking time: 45 minutes
♥ ✓ WF DF GF V

9 whole raw **beets** (about 1¾ lb)
10g **carrots** (about 1¾ lb)
¼ cup **extra virgin olive oil**
1½ tablespoons **honey**
1 tablespoon **balsamic vinegar**
¾ cup **slivered almonds**
3 tablespoons **fresh chervil** or **parsley leaves**—optional
sea salt and **freshly ground black pepper**

1. Preheat the oven to 400°F.

2. Peel the beets and cut them into substantial chunks. Peel the carrots and cut them into batons.

3. Put the beets and carrots into separate ovenproof dishes, coat with olive oil, and season well with salt and pepper. Add the honey to the carrots and the balsamic to the beets and stir well.

4. Put both dishes into the oven for 45 minutes, or until the carrots are starting to brown and the beets are soft.

5. Meanwhile, toast the almonds in a dry skillet over medium heat on the stove, being careful not to burn them. Chop the parsley, if using.

6. Place the cooked vegetables on a serving dish. Sprinkle with the chervil or parsley and the almonds.

 TIPS

○ This would go well with plain yogurt or some hummus and warm bread.

PURPLE BABY BROCCOLI *with beans & hazelnuts*

With the beans adding protein, this makes a great dinner on its own; the red onion adds sweetness, the nuts give crunch. Make sure you cook the broccoli until it is soft enough to soak up all the savory flavors (pictured on page 51).

Feeds: 4 as a side, 2 as a main
Preparation time: 10 minutes
Cooking time: 15 minutes
♥ ✓ WF DF GF

1 lb **purple baby broccoli**
⅛ cup whole peeled **hazelnuts**
4 cloves of **garlic**
½ (2 oz) can of **anchovies**
⅛ cup **extra virgin olive oil**
1 **red onion**
1 (2 oz) can of **great Northern beans**, drained
½ a **lemon**
sea salt and **freshly ground black pepper**

RECIPE TESTED BY CLAUDIA B.

1. Put a saucepan of salted water on to boil. Trim off the woody stems from the broccoli. Break up the hazelnuts by placing in a clean dish towel and bashing with a rolling pin, or coarsely chop them in a food processor. Toast the hazelnuts in a dry skillet over high heat, and set aside.

2. Peel and coarsely chop the garlic. Chop the anchovies. Heat the olive oil in a nonstick skillet, add the garlic, and cook for a minute. Peel and chop the onions into semicircles, and add them to the garlic along with the anchovies.

3. Toss the onions over high heat for 2 minutes. Turn the heat down to medium and cook for another 5–10 minutes, or until the onions are soft. Season well with salt and pepper, then add the beans, allowing them to just heat through.

4. Blanch the broccoli in the boiling water for 4 minutes (we like it a bit on the well cooked side for this dish), and drain. Arrange the broccoli on a big plate and sprinkle with the bean and onion mixture. Squeeze the juice of half a lemon over the vegetables and sprinkle the toasted hazelnuts on top before serving.

 TIPS

○ You can use many other green vegetables as the base—broccoli, kale, or green beans would all work. If you use everyday broccoli, just slice off the woody end and use the peeled stem as well as the florets. Waste not, want not.

○ You can substitute any type of bean for the great Northern beans.

○ For vegetarians, use capers instead of anchovies.

JOSSY'S BURMESE SPICY CABBAGE

All over Burma you find variations of both cabbage and cauliflower served in this way, with a lot of health-giving turmeric and ginger—great on rice or as a side dish.

Jossy on the beach in Lanzarote, 1973

Feeds: 4 (as a side dish)
Preparation time: 15 minutes
Cooking time: 7 minutes

♥ ✓ WF DF GF

1 small head of **green cabbage**
1 inch piece of **fresh ginger**
3 large cloves of **garlic**
½ cup roasted unsalted **peanuts**—optional
1 level teaspoon **turmeric**
juice of ½ a **lemon**
1 tablespoon **Thai fish sauce**
2 tablespoons **peanut oil**
a large handful of **fresh cilantro leaves**, coarsely chopped

I first tasted a dish like this at a stall on a Rangoon street in 1981. Jossy

1. Slice the cabbage as thinly as you can. Peel the ginger and garlic and slice both into the thinnest possible slivers. If using peanuts, chop finely.

2. Pour ½ cup of hot water into a small bowl, add the turmeric, and stir until smooth, then add the lemon juice and fish sauce.

3. Heat the peanut oil in a wok over medium heat, then add the sliced cabbage and stir for a minute or two, or until it just begins to soften.

4. Now add the slivers of ginger and garlic along with the chopped peanuts and continue stirring around for another 2–3 minutes.

5. Pour in the turmeric liquid. Stir over the heat for another minute or so, and throw in the cilantro leaves just before serving.

TIPS

○ Add another squeeze of lemon juice if you feel it needs an extra lift once you have tasted it.

○ A teaspoon of chili powder and some sesame seeds also make good additions.

○ It is a good dish to eat on its own with some rice or other vegetables, but would also be nice with some very simple broiled chicken.

Some words about Jossy by Henry

Being the offspring of a cookbook writer is a privilege. I didn't learn to cook at Mom's elbow—she was always busy making notes and would shoo me and my sisters out of the kitchen. But I learned to eat. Meal after meal we were the guinea pigs for experiments with new dishes that she had picked up at home and abroad. (The stepdaughter of a diplomat, she was brought up in Syria and Peru and never lost her touch with spices.)

When John, Allegra, and I opened Leon she would be there several times a week, tasting, making notes, and giving advice. And again with this book, she has been invaluable, testing recipes and suggesting ideas. She even offered some fast recipes of her own.

So if you see a recipe with this mark, *Jossy* you will know it is one of hers.
Thanks Mom.

MAIL
ION

FRIENDS & FAMILY RECIPES

ITALIAN FAVA BEANS

An easy and delicious standby dish. Serve it either hot with broiled chicken, fish, or meat, or as part of a cold meal, dribbled with olive oil.

Feeds: 4 (as a side)
Preparation time: 5 minutes
Cooking time: 15 minutes
♥ ✓ WF DF GF V

2–3 large cloves of **garlic**
1 (14½ oz) can of **diced tomatoes**
2 tablespoons **extra virgin olive oil**
2½ cups frozen **fava beans**
a small handful of fresh **basil leaves**
sea salt and **freshly ground black pepper**

1. Peel the garlic and slice into thin slivers.

2. Put the tomatoes, garlic, and olive oil into a heavy saucepan and season generously with salt and black pepper.

3. Bring to bubbling point and add the fava beans.

4. Bring the mixture to a boil again, then reduce the heat and simmer gently in the open pan for 10–15 minutes, or until the sauce has reduced and any liquid has evaporated.

5. Add the basil leaves, check the seasoning, and serve.

TIPS

o For extra depth of flavor, sauté a finely chopped slice of bacon or a couple of anchovies in the pan at the start, before you add the tomatoes.

PRIORITY
I had something like this in a stone house at the top of an Umbrian mountain on a family vacation, and realized what an easy standby dish it would be. *Jossy*

FRIENDS & FAMILY RECIPES

From the top: Italian Fava Beans; Carrot Puree;
Flash-Fried Zucchini with Green Sauce

CARROT PUREE

Good comfort food, and excellent with roasted chicken; it tastes astonishingly good for something so simple (pictured on page 56).

Feeds: 4 (as a side dish)
Preparation time: 10 minutes
Cooking time: 30 minutes
✓ WF GF V

12 **carrots** (about 1¾ lb)
2 tablespoons **butter**
1 whole **nutmeg**
sea salt and **freshly ground black pepper**

1. Put a saucepan of salted water on the stove to boil.

2. Cut the carrots into large chunks, put them into the pan, and cook for 30 minutes, or until soft.

3. Drain the carrots and let stand in a colander for 2 minutes to dry out.

4. Put them into a food processor, add the butter, and process until entirely smooth.

5. Grate in nutmeg to taste. Season.

- Make sure the carrots are properly cooked and soft, otherwise they won't blend to a smooth consistency.

- This puree is particularly good with simple broiled lamb chops.

- If you want to be healthy, you can use olive oil in place of the butter. If you want to be superluxurious, you can add more butter and some cream.

- You can puree almost any vegetable with butter and nutmeg like this and get results. Particularly good are parsnips or celeriac with game or beef, and Brussels sprouts, which you can puree in advance to save time on Christmas Day.

FLASH-FRIED ZUCCHINI *with green sauce*

Feeds: 4
Preparation time: 5 minutes
Cooking time: 5 minutes
♥ ✓ WF DF GF

4–5 **zucchini** (about 1½ lb)
3 cloves of **garlic**
¼ cup **extra virgin olive oil**
sea salt and **freshly ground black pepper**
a drizzle of **Green Sauce** (recipe on page 141)

1. Slice the zucchini on the diagonal about ½ inch thick. Finely chop the garlic.

2. Heat the oil in a large heavy skillet. Add the zucchini and cook fast until they start to brown (about 4 minutes). Add the garlic a minute before serving. Toss vigorously. Season well.

3. Serve immediately and drizzle with Green Sauce (see picture on page 56).

JOHN'S BROCCOLI *with garlic, cashew nuts & chile*

Feeds: 4
Preparation time: 5 minutes
Cooking time: 10 minutes
♥ ✓ WF DF GF V

1 bunch of **broccoli**
3 cloves of **garlic**
2 fresh **red chiles**
2 tablespoons **canola oil** or
   peanut oil
a small handful of **cashew nuts**
a hearty splash of **light soy sauce**
1 **lime**, cut into quarters

1. Cut the broccoli into medium florets
   and steam them lightly over boiling
   water so that they are partly cooked.

2. Peel and finely slice the garlic and
   chiles. Put them into a large skillet
   over medium heat with the
   canola or peanut oil and
   sauté until starting to soften.

3. Add the cashew nuts and broccoli
   and stir well, so that everything is
   coated with oil and golden garlic.

4. Add the soy sauce, cover with a lid,
   and cook for another 2 minutes.

5. Finish with a squeeze of lime.

 TIPS

○ This can be turned into a more substantial
   dish for 4 people by adding 2 fillets of salmon.

IMMEDIATE

I cooked this dish (with the salmon) a few
months ago when I was in need of a quick
lunch, and used pretty much everything
I had in the kitchen at the time. I sat back
to eat it at my desk and really enjoyed the
next ten minutes of eating pleasure.
The combination of chiles, soy sauce, and
cashews helped make this very healthy dish
a triumph of flavor. Simple and speedy.
John

IMMEDIATE

JOANNA'S PURPLE BABY BROCCOLI
with sausage & fennel

RECIPE TESTED BY: LUCY G & TOBY

Feeds: 4
Preparation time: 10 minutes
Cooking time: 20 minutes
✓ WF DF (GF if the sausages are GF)

Our friend Joanna Weinburg taught us how to make this. Dinner or lunch in just one bowl, with a surprising depth of flavor for such a simple dish.

4 cloves of **garlic**
1 tablespoon **extra virgin olive oil**
½ teaspoon **dried red pepper flakes**
2 teaspoons **fennel seeds**
1¾ lb plain best-quality **pork bulk sausage**
(or sausages, squeezed out of their skins)
1¾ lb **purple baby broccoli**
juice of 1 **lemon**

1. Peel and coarsely chop the garlic, then heat the oil in a skillet and gently sauté the red pepper flakes, garlic, and fennel seeds until the garlic is golden.

2. Crumble in the bulk sausage, turning it well in the mixture and breaking it up. Cook until the bottom becomes golden, then turn and break up again.

3. Chop the broccoli coarsely and add to the skillet. Turn well to coat it in the oil. Partly cover the dish and let cook for 5–7 minutes. The broccoli will still be crunchy.

4. Stir again, squeeze with the lemon juice, divide among plates, and eat immediately.

I first ate this dish in New York when I was living in a tiny apartment with no natural light (as you do), above the extractor fan of an Italian restaurant (as you do) called Il Bagatto on the Lower East Side. They made a version of this dish with *broccoli di rape*, a wonderfully bitter green that is quite difficult to find. It takes me right back to the exciting hum of Manhattan living. **Joanna**

Joanna Weinberg, 1974

FRIENDS & FAMILY RECIPES

TIPS

○ It works wonderfully with purple baby broccoli, but you could try it with kale, too.

○ The key is to use a large skillet so you have plenty of room to break up the sausage meat and brown it. If the skillet is too crowded, it will steam instead, and steamed sausage meat will not make anyone happy. Use sausage with a high meat content. Great served with crusty bread, preferably sourdough.

FRED'S ASPARAGUS

Fred and his friend Andy Weller, 2010

A very simple way with asparagus.

Feeds: 4
Preparation time: 5 minutes
Cooking time: 5–10 minutes

♥ ✓ WF DF GF V

1¼ lb **asparagus**
a medium handful of **fresh parsley**
a medium handful of **fresh tarragon**
2 tablespoons **extra virgin olive oil**
sea salt and **freshly ground black pepper**

FRIENDS & FAMILY
RECIPES

1. Snap off the woody ends the asparagus and rinse well.

2. Place the whole asparagus spears on a ridged grill pan or skillet, and cook for 5–10 minutes over low heat. There is no need to add any water or oil.

2. Meanwhile, chop the parsley and tarragon finely, and mix together in a bowl with the olive oil, salt, and pepper.

3. Plate up your cooked asparagus, drizzle with the herb oil, and serve.

My brother Fred is almost 30 years younger than me and something of a carnivore. He likes to spend his Friday evenings hunting in the country for rabbits with his friends. He makes a mean rabbit stew. This is him in more vegetarian mode.
Henry

GREEN BEANS *with tapenade, tomatoes & golden garlic*

Perfect as part of a veggie dinner, or as a summer side with lamb, chicken, or fish.

Feeds: 6 (as a side dish)
Preparation time: 15 minutes
Cooking time: 15 minutes

♥ ✓ WF DF GF

(V if you use anchovy-free tapenade)

5 cloves of **garlic**
⅛ cup **extra virgin olive oil**
1 lb **Italian flat beans** or other **green beans**
3 **tomatoes**
4 level teaspoons **tapenade**
sea salt and **freshly ground black pepper**

1. Fill a saucepan with salted water and bring it to a boil.

2. Peel the garlic and chop coarsely. Heat 2 tablespoons of olive oil in a saucepan on medium heat. Cook the garlic until golden and pour into a small dish.

3. Cut the ends off the beans, cut them on the diagonal into long diamonds, and add them to the boiling water. Cook until tender, drain, then dress with 2 tablespoons of olive oil and 2 teaspoons of tapenade. Season and spread on a plate.

4. Heat 2 tablespoons of olive oil in a very hot skillet. Coarsely chop the tomatoes into ½ inch cubes and throw them in. Season with salt, pepper, and the remaining 2 teaspoons of tapenade. Cook vigorously for a couple of minutes, until softened.

5. Heap the tomato and tapenade mixture into the center of the beans, sprinkle with the golden garlic, and serve.

TIPS

○ Don't worry about cooking the beans too crisp. Softer veg absorb more flavor.

○ You can substitute almost any type of greens for the green beans.

Above: Green Beans with Tapenade, Tomatoes & Golden Garlic; Below: Fred's Asparagus with Herb Oil

Hoppy's LEEKS VINAIGRETTE

Leeks vinaigrette is a classic vegetable dish, and Simon Hopkinson does it best—the vinaigrette itself is unsurpassed. This is an adaptation of his recipe.

Feeds: 4
Preparation time: 10 minutes
Cooking time: 15 minutes

♥ ✓ WF DF GF V

8 large **leeks** (about 3¼ lb)
1 tablespoon **Dijon mustard**
1 tablespoon **red wine vinegar**
⅔ cup **peanut oil** or other flavorless oil
1 tablespoon **chopped fresh chives**
2 tablespoons **capers**
sea salt and **freshly ground black pepper**

1. Trim the leeks, slice each one down the middle lengthwise (leaving the bottom attached to keep the two halves together), and wash thoroughly in warm water to remove any dirt.

2. Bring a large saucepan of salted water to a boil. Add the leeks and cook them for around 15 minutes, or until they are tender.

3. Put the mustard, vinegar, and 2 tablespoons of water into a blender or food processor and blend. With the machine still running, gradually add the oil until all the ingredients are homogenized. Season with salt and pepper. Add a little water if you think the dressing is too thick.

4. Drain the leeks well in a colander. Let cool a little, then cut off the bottom so that they separate into halves. Arrange neatly in a serving dish, cut sides downward. Drizzle with the dressing.

5. Chop the capers and sprinkle them over the leeks, with the chopped chives.

TIPS

○ It is essential that you don't use olive oil for this dish. As Simon says: "The dressing is important—and a good one, too, if I might say—as it not only doesn't use olive oil, but is all the better for it being omitted from a salad dressing, for once; oh! the ubiquity of that particular lotion, these days, delicious as it surely is …"

○ Simon serves his leeks with a chopped hard-boiled egg on top instead of capers.

○ Parsley can be used instead of chives.

○ This can be made well in advance. It gets better as the vinaigrette seeps into the leeks. If you serve it from the refrigerator, make sure you let it warm up for an hour or so at room temperature, because cold food doesn't have much flavour.

○ This is great as a light dinner, with some sourdough toast and a poached egg.

Simon has been an inspiration to me
from a young age. He is a chef who
loves eating (not as common as it
might seem). A wholesome greediness
and a generosity of spirit permeate
his books. The food is simple but—as
he proves with this vinaigrette—he
always gets the proportions just right
to create something sensational.
Henry

FRIENDS & FAMILY
RECIPES

ROASTED VEG TIPS

The Chevrolet of roasted vegetable dishes—generally picked up during student days—usually involves chopping a random selection of vegetables into chunks of military regularity and throwing them into a roasting pan with some oil, salt, and pepper. Back then, if we were feeling flamboyant, we might add some fluffy dice or a beaded car-seat cover in the form of vinegar or a sprig of rosemary. And very nice they were too, thank you very much. With a little more care, however, it is possible to create something quite sophisticated. Here's how:

- o **Choose your ingredients wisely.** Don't just throw in everything you have on hand. Two or three vegetables that go well together will be much more satisfying. Likewise, think about what herb or spice will add that perfect burst of flavor instead of reaching for the rosemary every time.

- o **Think about the look as well as the taste.** We eat first with our eyes, and cutting vegetables elegantly makes them more alluring. It can also affect the flavor—cutting parsnips thinly, for example, creates maximum golden gooeyness.

- o **Play with texture.** Whether it is crunch in the form of nuts, or a crispy topping of Parmesan and bread crumbs, a little texture lifts the dish to the next level.

ROASTED PARSNIPS & CARROTS *with honey & fennel seeds*

The carrots and parsnips in this recipe are cut into long strips so they turn a nice golden color.

Feeds: 4
Preparation time: 10 minutes
Cooking time: 40 minutes

♥ ✓ WF DF GF V

8 **carrots**
5 **parsnips**
2 heaping tablespoons **honey**
2 tablespoons **olive oil**
2 teaspoons **fennel seeds**
sea salt and **freshly ground black pepper**

1. Preheat the oven to 375°F.

2. Chop the carrots and parsnips into long elegant strips and put into a large roasting pan.

3. Add the honey, oil, fennel seeds, and seasoning, and mix together roughly with your hands.

4. Cook in the oven for 40 minutes, or until tender and golden.

TIPS

- o Some whole cloves of garlic make a good addition.

Clockwise from the top: Roasted Carrots & Fennel in Parmesan Bread Crumbs; Mediterranean Roasted Vegetables; Parsnips & Carrots with Honey & Fennel Seeds

MEDITERRANEAN ROASTED VEGETABLES

Summery roasted vegetables, served with green sauce and great with grilled meat or fish (pictured on page 67).

Feeds: 4 (as a side)
Preparation time: 5 minutes
Cooking time: 45 minutes

· ♥ ✓ WF DF GF V

2 small **eggplants**, or 1 large
2 **zucchini**
12 **cherry tomatoes**
⅛ cup **olive oil**
2 tablespoons **white wine vinegar**
½ cup **pine nuts**
sea salt and **freshly ground black pepper**

1. **Preheat the oven to 400°F.**

2. **Cut the ends off the eggplants and slice them thinly lengthwise, from top to bottom. Cut the zucchini into batons, and halve the tomatoes.**

3. **Put the eggplants into an ovenproof dish and spread the zucchini and tomatoes over the top.**

4. **Sprinkle with the olive oil and vinegar, and season with salt and pepper. Place the dish in the oven to cook for 45 minutes.**

5. **Sprinkle the pine nuts over the vegetables 5 minutes before you are ready to take them out of the oven, so that they can brown. Be careful they don't burn.**

6. **Drizzle with a few spoonfuls of Green Sauce (page 141) and serve.**

 TIPS

○ Cooking times may vary a little, depending on the kind of dish or oven pan you are using, so use a little common sense to prevent the vegetables from either burning, or being undercooked, which is always unpleasant when eating eggplants.

Souvenir from Mallorca, 1976

ROASTED CARROTS & FENNEL *in Parmesan bread crumbs*

A crisp and scented alternative to traditional roasted vegetables (pictured on page 67).

Feeds: 4
Preparation time: 15 minutes
Cooking time: 35 minutes

♥ ✓ V

6 **carrots**
1 lbg **fennel**
a large bunch of **fresh rosemary**
¼ cup **extra virgin olive oil**
2–3 slices **stale white bread**
3 cloves of **garlic**
½ cup freshly grated **Parmesan cheese**
sea salt and **freshly ground black pepper**

1. Preheat your oven as high as it will go.

2. Peel the carrots and cut into ½ inch diagonal disks. Trim the fennel and cut into long elegant wedges (cut each bulb in half, then into 8–10 slices, depending on thickness). Pick the leaves off the rosemary.

3. Put the vegetables into a large roasting pan. Add the olive oil and ½ cup of water. Place on the top shelf of the oven for 20 minutes, turning after 10 minutes.

4. Put the bread, rosemary leaves, garlic, salt, and pepper into the blender, and process until fine.

5. Once the carrots and fennel are cooked (the carrots should have some bite and the fennel should be translucent), sprinkle the bread crumb mixture over them and top with the Parmesan.

6. Put back into the oven for another 15 minutes.

TIPS

- If you don't have any stale bread, you can use fine couscous instead.
  Simply prinkle it over the vegetables, along with the finely grated Parmesan, and roast as usual.

- You can make stale bread by putting small chunks of fresh bread into the oven for 10 minutes at 225°F.

- Use a micrograter to grate the Parmesan for an extra fine and crunchy topping.

QUICK SOUPS

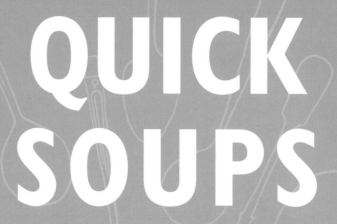

Gandhi said, "Drink your food and chew your drink." He might have been onto something. A lot of recent studies have shown that eating soup is a quick route to svelte thighs and a small but healthy belly.

In our restaurants, the soups change every day and reflect the seasons. This gives us plenty of opportunity for being adventurous with new dishes. Some of the soups in this section are from the restaurants, others are from our family recipe books.

JERUSALEM ARTICHOKE SOUP

Feeds: 4
Preparation time: 25 minutes
Cooking time: 55 minutes

✓ WF GF

2¼ lb **Jerusalem artichokes**
lemon juice
1 large **onion**
2 tablespoons **butter**
4 cups **whole milk**
1 **chicken bouillon cube**
1 tablespoon **chopped fresh flat-leaf parsley**
sea salt and **freshly ground black pepper**

1. Peel and chop the artichokes, and put them in a saucepan of water with a squeeze of lemon juice to stop them from turning brown.

2. Peel and chop the onion.

3. Heat the butter in a saucepan and sauté the onion and artichokes until soft, not brown.

4. Add the milk and crumble in the bouillon cube. Stir well and simmer for 35–45 minutes.

5. When cool enough, process in a blender until smooth and reheat to serve.

6. Season with salt and pepper and sprinkle with the parsley. You could add a swirl of heavy cream if you desire, too.

Leon (right) in the RAF, Cyprus 1958

ZUCCHINI SOUP

This soup is equally good hot or cold, depending on the season.

Feeds: 4
Preparation time: 5 minutes
Cooking time: 40 minutes
♥ ✓ WF GF

4 **zucchini**
1 large **onion**
2 tablespoons **butter**
3 cups **chicken stock**
sea salt and **freshly ground black pepper**

1. Trim and slice the zucchini. Finely chop the onion.

2. Melt the butter in a large saucepan. Add the onion and sauté gently for about 5 minutes, or until soft but not brown.

3. Add the zucchini, stir for a minute, then add the stock and bring to a boil. Cover and simmer gently for 30 minutes.

4. Process with an electric mixer or in a food processor and season with salt and pepper. Serve hot, or cold from the refrigerator in summer.

FRIENDS & FAMILY RECIPES

My grandmother made the most delicious soups, despite lacking the patience to make real stock. In 1994, she wrote out all her recipes for me by hand. There was, she assured me, no need to go hunting around for "nonsensical sprigs of unobtainable herbs": a bouillon chicken stock cube and a handful of veg ("preferably fresh") was all anyone needed for a feast.
Mima

Mima and Hattie with their parents and grandparents, 1977

Zucchini Soup (above) and
Jerusalem Artichoke Soup

JOSSY'S MYSTERY SOUP

So called because nobody ever guesses what this creamy pale green soup is made from, and although you may think the combination of ingredients sounds doubtful, it's delicious, and good hot or chilled.

Feeds: 4 as a main,
6 as an appetizer
Preparation time: 5 minutes
Cooking time: 15 minutes

✓ WF GF

1 lb thin **leeks**
2 **chicken bouillon cubes**
1 large ripe **avocado**
juice of ½ a small **lemon**
⅔ cup **heavy cream**
a large handful of **fresh flat-leaf parsley**
sea salt and **cayenne pepper**

1. Prepare the leeks and slice across them finely, using as much of the green part as possible.

2. Pour 5 cups of water into a saucepan, crumble in the bouillon cubes, and stir over medium heat until dissolved. Bring to a boil, add the sliced leeks, cover the pan, and simmer for 8–10 minutes, or until the leeks are soft.

3. Meanwhile, cut the avocado in half, scoop out the flesh, and put it into a food processor with the lemon juice and cream. Process until very smooth. Chop the parsley very finely.

4. Add the avocado puree to the leeks and stir to mix evenly.

5. Bring the soup to a boil again for just a minute, then stir in the chopped parsley and remove from the heat.

6. Season with salt and cayenne pepper.

 TIPS

○ If you're not intending to eat it at once and need to reheat the soup later, remove it from the heat immediately when it begins to bubble.

From the top: Mystery Soup; Lima Bean Soup with Roasted Peppers & Sautéed Garlic; Belinda's Chicken Noodle Soup

LIMA BEAN SOUP *with roasted peppers & sautéed garlic*

Lima beans make a wonderfully smooth and soothing soup, but this one has great kick and texture, too (pictured on page 75).

Feeds: 4–5
Preparation time: 15 minutes
Cooking time: 10 minutes

✓ WF GF V

Jossy

1 large **red bell pepper**
2 (15 oz) cans of **lima beans**
5 tablespoons unsalted **butter**
2½ cups **whole milk**
4 large cloves of **garlic**
2 tablespoons **olive oil**
2–4 pinches of **chili powder** or **dried red pepper flakes**
juice of 1 **lemon**
sea salt

1. Quarter the bell pepper lengthwise and discard the seeds and stem.

2. Lay the bell pepper pieces skin side upward on a piece of aliminum foil under a hot broiler. Remove when the skin has blackened and wrap the pepper in the foil until cool enough to handle. Peel off the black skin and cut the pepper pieces into very thin strips.

3. Drain the lima beans and put them into a food processor or blender with 3 tablespoons of butter at room temperature. Add a tablespoon of milk and process until smooth, gradually adding the rest of the milk. Season with salt.

4. Peel the garlic and slice the cloves across thinly. Put the olive oil and the remaining butter into a large saucepan over fairly high heat and add the garlic and red pepper flakes. Stir for just a minute or two, or until golden brown—don't let the garlic burn. Add the lima bean mixture and simmer for 2 minutes. Remove from the heat, gradually stir in the lemon juice, and add the strips of roasted pepper.

TIPS

○ Try this with anchovies added to the garlic, red pepper flakes, and oil. It gives a fantastic extra kick and dimension to the soup.

FRIENDS & FAMILY RECIPES

BELINDA'S CHICKEN NOODLE SOUP

A quick and healthy week-night dinner (pictured on page 75).

Feeds: 4
Preparation time: 10 minutes
Cooking time: 10 minutes

♥ ✓ WF DF GF

4 cups **chicken stock**
2 **chicken breasts**
2 cloves of **garlic**
8 oz mixed shiitake and cremini **mushrooms**
4 oz **bok choy**
a large handful of **fresh cilantro**
2 tablespoons **peanut oil**
8 oz **rice noodles**
3 tablespoons **soy sauce**
2 tablespoons **toasted sesame oil**

1. Put the chicken stock into a saucepan, put a lid on, and bring to a boil. Cut the chicken breasts into small chunks.

2. Peel and finely slice the garlic. Generously slice the mushrooms. Coarsely chop the bok choy and cilantro.

3. Pour the peanut oil into a hot wok or wide, heavy saucepan. When it smokes, add the garlic just for seconds and immediately follow with the chicken and mushrooms. Keep tossing until cooked (about 5–7 minutes). Add the soy sauce and sesame oil and keep tossing until absorbed.

4. Add the rice noodles and bok choy to the hot chicken stock, put a lid on, and boil for 3–4 minutes. Pour the contents of the wok into the pan of stock and noodles and sprinkle with the cilantro. Eat immediately.

| TIPS |

o   Depending on what brand of rice noodles you use, you may need to add extra stock—some soak up more juice than others.

o   A squeeze of lime on top before you eat is a nice addition.

Belinda, my stepmother, appears effortlessly to combine managing a large extended family, a doctorate, and a new career in psychology with the production of enormous feasts whenever family and friends descend upon her house (which is quite often). This is one of her staple meals.
Henry

Belinda at Picnic Point, summer 2009

FRIENDS & FAMILY RECIPES

BACON AND ROOT VEG SOUP

A winter warmer and a Mima staple.

Feeds: 4–6
Preparation time: 20 minutes
Cooking time: 30 minutes

✓ WF GF

4 oz **bacon**
1 large **onion**
2 large **carrots**
½ **rutabaga** or 1 **sweet potato**
3 Yukon gold or white round **potatoes**
3 **parsnips**
2 tablespoons **olive oil**
2 **bay leaves**
6½ cups **chicken stock**
1 cup grated **cheddar or Parmesan cheese**
sea salt and **freshly ground black pepper**

1. Cut the bacon into small pieces. Peel and chop the onion. Peel and dice the carrots, rutabaga, potatoes, and parsnips.

2. Heat the oil in a heavy saucepan. Add the bacon and cook until it is just getting crispy. Add the onion, and cook until it is getting soft.

3. Add all the diced vegetables and the bay leaves, and cook over gentle heat with the lid on for 10 minutes, stirring occasionally.

4. Add the stock and simmer for 15 minutes, or until the vegetables are tender.

5. Remover and discard the bay leaves. Season with salt and pepper and serve in bowls, sprinkled with the cheese.

- Vegetarians can use garlic instead of the bacon, and vegetable stock instead of chicken stock.

- You can use any surplus root vegetables you have lying about. Celeriac tastes great alongside or instead of the parsnip.

APPLE'S PERSIAN ONION SOUP

A favorite recipe from the restaurants—very healthy, and great if you are feeling under par.

Feeds: 4 as an appetizer
Preparation time: 10 minutes
Cooking time: 40 minutes

♥ ✓ WF DF GF

4 large **onions**
2 tablespoons **olive oil**
1 heaping teaspoon **turmeric**
1 heaping teaspoon **ground fenugreek**
1 teaspoon **dried mint**
4 cups **chicken** or **vegetable stock**
1 **cinnamon stick**
½ a **lemon**
sea salt and **freshly ground black pepper**

1. Peel the onions and slice thinly. Put the onions into a large saucepan with the olive oil. Add some salt and pepper, cover the pan, and cook gently for at least 15 minutes, stirring occasionally.

2. Add the turmeric, fenugreek, and mint, and cook for another few minutes without the lid.

3. Add the stock and cinnamon stick, bring to a boil, then reduce the heat and simmer for at least 20 minutes.

4. Add the juice of half a lemon, season with salt and pepper, and serve. I like to leave the cinnamon stick in.

TIPS

o Add some chopped fresh mint and parsley at the end to liven things up.

o Apple adds a teaspoon of sugar for added sweetness—we leave this out.

Apple and Sophie Douglas Bate pretending to be supermodels, 2001

My best pal Sophie Douglas Bate is the most incredible chef from Edible Food Design, and we have cooked and traveled together for years. Her family used to live in Tehran and this became a staple soup in our lives—great for when you are trying to lose weight.
Apple

FRIENDS & FAMILY RECIPES

SOUP LIFTERS

Like a striking brooch on "that old" outfit, finishing touches have the power to transform a dish. If your soup is feeling a bit flat, don't lose heart. Season it carefully and lift it with one of these toppers.

Mushroom duxelle

Crispy garlic bread crumbs

Sliced pecans

Cilantro

Seeds and herbs

Rose Harissa

Crispy fried sage

Crispy parsnips

Yogurt

Melted onions

Roasted peppers

Scallions

Herb butter

Golden fried garlic

Pesto

Crème fraîche

Crispy bacon

Turkish red pepper flakes

Grated cheddar

Finely chopped zucchini and carrot

Parsley

Grated Parmesan

Toasted almonds

Lemon zest

RICE, POTATOES, COUSCOUS & QUINOA

THREE QUICK WAYS WITH RICE

For some reason, rice seems to cause cooks an unwarranted amount of stress. Here are three supersimple ways to ease your rice-furrowed brow.

 1 FAIL-SAFE RICE Absorption method

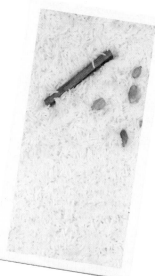

Use white basmati rice.

1. Rinse the rice thoroughly in a strainer (use about ½ cup per person, but if you make extra you can use it to make Michelle's saffron rice cake, below).

2. Use EXACTLY 1¼ cups of water to 1 cup of rice. Put into a saucepan and bring to a boil.

3. Immediately turn the heat down to the lowest possible setting and cover the pan with a tight-fitting lid. It will take about 15 minutes to cook, but you can turn off the heat and leave it with the lid on for up to 40 minutes before serving.

 TIPS

○ You do not need to add salt to the rice, but a squeeze of lemon and some butter at the end make a great seasoning.

○ You can put a little oil or butter into the pan before you add the rice and gently sauté a cinnamon stick with a couple of crushed cardamom pods to add an aromatic flavor. Add turmeric at this stage if you want orange rice.

 2 *Michelle's* **CRISPY SAFFRON RICE CAKE**

A simple recipe for leftover rice. Basmati works best, but you can use any kind.

1. Heat a generous pat of butter in a nonstick saucepan or skillet, and add a good pinch of saffron (if saffron seems a bit expensive, a pinch of turmeric will work, too).

2. Add enough rice to cover the bottom of the pan, and pack it down well. Add the rest of the rice. With a chopstick or skewer, make 3 holes to let the steam escape. Cover the rice with paper towels and a lid and put the pan over low heat.

3. Let cook for 10 minutes over low to medium heat until the bottom is crispy, and then turn out onto a plate.

4. The rice should be crisp on the bottom, and you should be able to turn it out onto a plate in a cake shape.

Michelle at home in London, 1979

3 PILAF

There is possibly nothing more comforting than pilaf—eat it as a side dish or as a simple dinner on its own. This all-in-the-oven version is almost impossibly easy.

Feeds: 4
Preparation time: 5 minutes
Cooking time: 45 minutes
♥ ✓ WF DF GF

4 large **carrots**
2 **onions**
3 tablespoons **olive oil**
2 cups short-grain brown or white **rice**
3½ cups **chicken** or **vegetable stock**
3 **bay leaves**, fresh or dried
juice of ½ a **lemon**
a large handful of **fresh parsley**
sea salt and **freshly ground black pepper**

1. Preheat the oven to 350°F. Peel the carrots and cut them into batons. Peel the onions and slice them into semicircles.

2. Put the carrots and onions into a large ovenproof dish and add the oil, stirring to coat the vegetables. Place in the oven and cook for 20 minutes, making sure the onions don't burn.

3. Meanwhile, measure out the rice and heat your stock. Coarsely chop the parsley.

4. Add the rice and bay leaves to the dish of vegetables and cover with the hot stock. The rice should be well covered, but not swimming in too much liquid.

5. Return the dish to the oven and cook for another 25 minutes, checking regularly to make sure the rice does not cook dry. Add extra stock if it needs it.

6. When the rice is cooked and has absorbed the liquid, it should have a wonderful risotto-ish texture. Add the lemon juice and chopped parsley and season well.

 **TIPS**

o Pilaf is always improved by a sprinkling of toasted slivered almonds (or any other nuts or seeds) over the top.

o You can use many other vegetables with this base recipe: sweet potatoes, garlic, bell peppers, chopped tomatoes, and zucchini, for example.

o Experiment with different herb and spice combinations with the vegetable mixture.

o Add chicken or slices of leftover lamb to make the dish more substantial.

o Succulent golden raisins always go well in a rice dish, if you like it slightly sweet.

o If you want to make it more like a risotto, you can use risotto rice. You may need to add up to 1 cup extra stock for this.

THREE QUICK WAYS WITH POTATOES

A simple boiled potato with a pat of butter and some black pepper is a glorious thing—but it's worth making some changes. Potatoes have so much more to give.

 ## 1 Baked in stock

Like scalloped potatoes, but without the cream. You can experiment with herb, spice, and vegetable combinations. The recipe below is one of our favorites.

POTATOES LEON-AISE

Feeds: 6 as a side
Preparation time: 10 minutes
Cooking time: 1 hour
♥ WF GF DF

12 white round **potatoes** (about 3 lb)
2 large **onions**
1 bulb of **garlic**
½ a **lemon**
5 **fresh bay leaves**
⅛ cup **extra virgin olive oil**
2¾ cups **chicken stock**
sea salt and **freshly ground black pepper**

1. Preheat the oven to 350°F.

2. Wash the potatoes thoroughly, and slice thinly with their skins still on.

3. Peel and slice the onions finely. Slice the garlic bulb thinly crosswise (leaving the skin on). Slice the lemon half as finely as you can muster.

4. Toss everything except the stock into a baking pan. Season well. Pat down so it fits snugly. Pour in the stock—it should come about halfway up the potatoes.

5. Place them in the oven for 1 hour, or until cooked.

 ## 2 Boiled, then dressed

Boil your potatoes as usual, but instead of a simple coating of butter and pepper, finish them with panache. The Warm Anchovy, Garlic & Potato Salad (page 158) is one example. Our two other favorites are:

Crispy Garlic and Ginger Let the potatoes steam dry in the colander, then sauté them in a skillet with chopped garlic and ginger until all the ingredients turn golden and crispy. (This is a great way to treat leftover cooked potatoes from the refrigerator.)

Tangy Parsley Sauce Melt some butter in a pan. Add finely chopped parsley and a dash of vinegar. Season and pour over the potatoes.

3 Chopped small and roasted

There are plenty of fast, delicious variations on Pierre's Potatoes (see page 135). The essential moves are: chop your raw potatoes small, put plenty of oil in a roasting pan, get it spitting hot in the oven before you add the potatoes, then put the pan back in and cook them fast and hot. These are some of our favorite embellishments:

Traditional Woody herbs and whole cloves of garlic.

Meaty Little chunks of chorizo or pieces of sausage.

Bay More fresh bay leaves than you would ever imagine (e.g. about 15 in baking pan).

Spanish Sweet paprika and sliced onions.

THREE QUICK WAYS WITH SWEET POTATOES

We have had a love affair with this sweet, soft tuber since we first opened our doors.

 ## ROASTED SWEET POTATOES

1. Preheat the oven to 350–400°F.

2. Cut your sweet potatoes into thick wedges with the skin on.
   Place them in a large baking pan.

3. Sprinkle with a tablespoon of ground cumin or ground coriander,
   or dried red pepper flakes (or all three).

4. Season with salt and pepper and toss in a generous dash of olive oil.

5. Put into the oven for 30 minutes, or until
   cooked and slightly crispy.

 ## ANDI'S SWEET POTATO FRIES

Finally, a healthy(ish) fry.

1. Finely slice your sweet potatoes into elegant
   slim batons, leaving the skins on.

2. Cook small batches in hot vegetable oil
   until golden.

3. Drain, scatter with sea salt, and eat immediately.

 ## BAKED SWEET POTATOES
with numerous stuffings

1. Heat the oven to around 350°F. Bake whole for
   around 1 hour, or until soft.

2. Split the potatoes open and stuff.

Stuffings we like include:

- Homemade hummus
- Tsatsiki
- Feta cheese and scallions
- Crème fraîche and za'tar
- Yogurt and harissa

Andi, Cyprus 1972

FRIENDS & FA
RECIPES

Andi lives around the corner from me in Hackney, London. She has a smile that could power a power plant and, man, can she cook. I had been trying and failing to get sweet potato fries to be crispy for months when she came around with this recipe to relieve my pain. The trick is to cut them very fine, cook them in hot, hot oil, and eat them immediately. *Henry*

Sweet potatoes are one of those vegetables (along with carrots) where buying organic makes a real difference to flavor. The tubers are smaller, more dense, and have a deep intensity of flavor.

Clockwise from the top: Roasted Sweet Potatoes; Andi's Sweet Potato Fries; Baked Sweet Potatoes

THREE QUICK WAYS WITH COUCOUS, BULGUR WHEAT, & QUINOA

Although the first two of these are forms of wheat and the latter is an unprocessed grain unto itself, you can use these three beauties interchangeably. Feel free to switch the grains in the recipes below. (If you don't fancy wheat, look for the traditional Moroccan barley couscous from online sources or health food stores.)

 Grain salads

1. Cook the grain as per the directions on the package. (For couscous and bulgur wheat, you can usually just pour over boiling stock or water and let soak, but quinoa will take a bit more cooking.)

2. Mix in olive oil, lemon juice, seasoning, and your choice of additional ingredients. We like pine nuts, dried apricots, arugula leaves, finely sliced red onion, and fresh parsley; or olives, flash-fried zucchini and eggplants, "Sun-dried" Tomatoes (see page 267) and fresh mint.

However, we have a particular soft spot for this recipe—and for its creator, our friend Laura.

LAURA'S JEWELED SALAD

Feeds: 4
Preparation time: 5 minutes
Cooking time: 5 minutes
♥ WF V

1 cup **barley couscous**
8 oz good-quality **feta cheese**
1 **cucumber**
a bunch of **mixed fresh green herbs,**
   e.g. **mint** and **cilantro**
¾ cup **pine nuts**
seeds of 1 large **pomegranate**
2 cloves of **garlic**
2 tablespoons **extra virgin olive oil**
juice of 1½ **lemons**
sea salt and **freshly ground black pepper**

Laura in her favorite party dress, 1987

1. Prepare the couscous as per the directions on the package. Let cool in a large bowl.

2. Crumble the feta and cut the cucumber into chunks. Add these to the bowl, then coarsely tear the herbs and add them, too.

3. Lightly toast the pine nuts in a skillet over low heat, and sprinkle these and the pomegranate seeds over the salad.

4. Peel and finely mince or grate the garlic. Whisk together the olive oil, lemon juice, and garlic and pour the dressing over the salad. Season well with salt and pepper, then serve.

FRIENDS & FAMILY
RECIPES

② Grain pilafs

For something a little more substantial, you can also treat your grains as you would rice in a pilaf. Simply roast any leftover vegetables you have, then cook them with the grains in stock. This recipe came to us via Henry's wife, Mima, whose sister Hattie picked it up from her friend Lucy, whose mother used to live in Cyprus. A typically picaresque recipe journey.

HATTIE'S POURGOURI

Feeds: 4
Preparation time: 5 minutes
Cooking time: 20 minutes
♥ DF V

2 small **onions** (or 1 large)
3 cloves of **garlic**
a handful of **fresh mint**, **flat-leaf parsley**, or **cilantro**
3 tablespoons **olive oil**
1¼ cups **bulgur wheat**
2 (14½ oz) cans of **diced tomatoes**
a handful of **almonds**, **pistachios**, or **pine nuts**
sea salt and **freshly ground black pepper**

1. Peel the onions and garlic and chop finely. Chop the herbs.

2. Heat the oil in a heavy saucepan. Add the onions and garlic and cook for 5 minutes.

3. Add the bulgur wheat, stir well, and add the diced tomatoes. Stir thoroughly and lower the heat. Put a lid on the pan and cook gently for 15 minutes, stirring regularly, because it can stick easily.

4. When the bulgur is soft, add salt, pepper, and the chopped herbs.

5. Toast the nuts in a skillet and sprinkle them over the top when you are ready to eat.

TIPS

o Drizzle with extra olive oil, if necessary.

o Delicious with Greek yogurt, and wonderful served with roasted lamb.

o As good cold as it is hot.

③ Grains in soups

Adding grains toward the end of cooking is a great way to bulk up your soups. You will need to add them at slightly different times before you serve them. As a guide:

o Couscous   less than 3 minutes

o Bulgur wheat 10 minutes

o Quinoa   15 minutes

Hattie's Pourgouri (above); Laura's Jeweled Salad (below)

MEAT AS A SIDE DISH

As we mentioned at the start of the vegetable section, it pays to think of the meat dish as a side to the vegetables instead of vice versa. Not in a bad way, you understand. Think of Elizabeth Taylor snuggled into the sidecar of a classic Triumph.

If you are concentrating your energies on the vegetables, you want to spend less time and money on the meat. Here are some ways that we go about that.

1 **Smash, dash, and flash**—A quick way to tackle a small amount of a cheaper cut of any meat. Slice into ½ inch thick slices, then wrap in plastic wrap and give it a good whack with a rolling pin until it is at least half the thickness. The thinner the better, because this is just meant to be a flash of taste, and thinly cut pieces of chicken, for example, can carry more flavor than a big chunk. Cut the pieces into credit-card-size pieces, and dip (or dash) them into a strong flavoring—e.g. a store-bought garam masala, curry powder, or Indian paste. Season with sea salt and freshly ground black pepper. Flash-fry or broil at a high heat for a minute or so on each side. Squeeze with some lemon before serving.

2 **Leftovers**—Buy a slightly bigger roast than you need for the weekend and you'll have meat side dishes for the next week. Chicken can be reheated in a little stock, with some frozen peas thrown in and Parmesan grated on top (see picture opposite). Leftover lamb makes a soothing pilaf (see page 87). And just about any leftover meat can be chopped finely and fried up with garlic and ginger paste and green herbs.

3 **A slice of sausage**—Buy a really good fresh chorizo and broil a little for the side. This also goes for standard sausages, which, sliced into ½ inch disks and fried until crisp with fennel seeds, make a great meat garnish (see picture opposite).

4 **Marvelous meals with ground meat**—Cook a little ground meat with some ground cumin, salt, and pepper in a saucepan until brown with some crispy bits. (If you like, add pine nuts, onions, and garlic). Sprinkle it over a canned bean salad, some green beans, or a prepared hummus. (You can use this same topper approach with little bits of bacon—great on fava beans—see picture—or broken-up sausage.)

5 **A good variety**—If you love variety meats, a whole other world of cheap and tasty meat is open to you. You can't beat the classics: "devilled" kidneys fried with Worcestershire sauce, butter, cayenne, and mustard (see opposite); or fried chicken livers with sherry vinegar and parsley.

6 **The white stuff**—It is still possible to buy fresh, sustainable white fish (like whiting and pollock)—check the Marine Stewardship Council's website for sustainable sources. But these need some flavor. Buy fillets and treat them as the meat above without the bashing.

There is a reason why curries have become the nation's favorite meals, and it's not just because they go so well with beer. The bold spices of Eastern cuisine can work miracles on just about any base ingredient, from chicken and fish to beans. Go easy on the ghee, and you'll find they make you healthy and beautiful, too.

QUICK CURRIES

COCONUT CHICKEN & *peas curry*

A fantastically quick curry to make.

Feeds: 4–6
Preparation time: 10 minutes
Cooking time: 15 minutes
✓ WF GF

6 **chicken breasts**
2 tablespoons **butter**
2 teaspoons **nigella seeds** (black onion seeds)
2 tablespoons **tikka paste**
1¼ cups **coconut milk**
1⅛ cups **frozen peas**
a handful of **fresh cilantro leaves**
sea salt and **freshly ground black pepper**

1. Slice the chicken breasts into thin strips.

2. Melt the butter in a heavy skillet. Add the chicken and nigella seeds and cook for between 8–10 minutes, or until the chicken is cooked through.

3. Stir in the tikka paste, coconut milk, and peas. Bring gently to a boil, stirring all the time, and simmer for a minute or two.

4. Chop the cilantro, add to the skillet and season with salt and pepper.

 TIPS

○ All the ingredients for this lightning recipe can be kept in your freezer or pantry, so grab the chicken on your way home and you can be eating a delicious creamy curry within minutes.

○ Basmati rice, which takes about 10 minutes to cook, or any freshly cooked long-grain rice completes the meal.

Clockwise from the top: Dalston Sweet Potato Curry: Coconut Chicken with Peas; Jossy's Chicken Liver Curry

After a visit to Vietnam decades ago, I longed for the comforting richness of coconut milk in my home cooking. However, at that time the only possibility was to laboriously make your own from fresh or dried coconut; these days cans are available for instant transformation to spicy dishes. Peas are found in so many Indian dishes that it is surprising no other cuisine seems to have realized how well they go with spices, and in my view the only way to enjoy chicken breasts is thinly sliced and strongly flavored.

Jossy

97

JOSSY'S CHICKEN LIVER CURRY

One for the liver lovers—tangy and meaty and very cheap (pictured on page 96).

Feeds: 4–6
Preparation time: 20 minutes
Cooking time: 35 minutes
✓ WF GF

1¾ lb **chicken livers**
3 tablespoons **plain yogurt**
2 medium **onions**
3 cloves of **garlic**
1 inch piece of **fresh ginger**
2 tablespoons **tikka paste**
3 tablespoons **lemon juice**
2 tablespoons **butter**
1 teaspoon **cumin seeds**
1 (14½ oz) can of **diced tomatoes**
a large handful of **fresh cilantro leaves**
sea salt and **freshly ground black pepper**

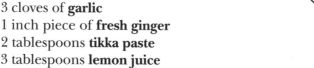

1. Cut the chicken livers into 1 inch pieces (removing any sinewy parts), place in a bowl, add the yogurt and set aside.

2. Peel the onions, garlic, and ginger and coarsely chop. Put one of the onions into a blender with the garlic, ginger, tikka paste, and lemon juice and process to a paste.

3. Transfer the mixture to a casserole dish, place over low heat, and simmer gently for about 15 minutes, stirring frequently.

4. Finely slice the remaining onion and add to the dish with the butter, cumin seeds, chicken livers, and tomatoes. Simmer for another 15 minutes, stirring occasionally.

5. Season with coarsely chopped cilantro and season with salt and pepper.

 TIPS

○ Best served with basmati rice and a salad.

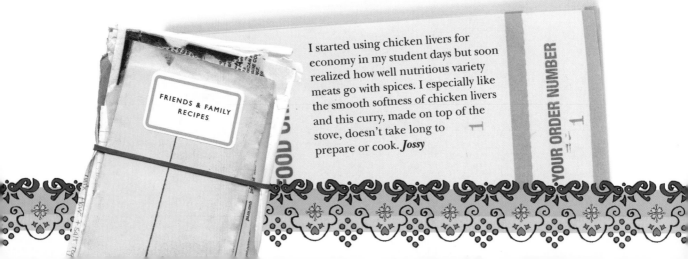

FRIENDS & FAMILY
RECIPES

I started using chicken livers for economy in my student days but soon realized how well nutritious variety meats go with spices. I especially like the smooth softness of chicken livers and this curry, made on top of the stove, doesn't take long to prepare or cook. *Jossy*

YOUR ORDER NUMBER
1

DALSTON SWEET POTATO CURRY

A sweet, rich, everyday vegetable curry (pictured on page 96).

Feeds: 6
Preparation time: 15 minutes
Cooking time: 40 minutes
✓ WF DF GF V

1 **onion**
1 tablespoon **sunflower oil**
4 cloves of **garlic**
1 inch piece of **fresh ginger**
2 teaspoons **ground coriander**
2 teaspoons **ground cumin**
½–1 teaspoon **cayenne pepper**, depending how hot you like it
1 level teaspoon **turmeric**
1 (14½ oz) can of **diced tomatoes**
4 **sweet potatoes** (not the giant ones)
1 **cauliflower**
1¾ cups **coconut milk**
1 cup **cashew nuts**
sea salt and **freshly ground black pepper**

1. Peel the onion, coarsely chop, and sauté gently in the oil in a large saucepan for 5 minutes. Peel and grate the garlic and ginger, add to the pan, and sauté for 1 minute. Add the spices and cook for another 2 minutes, until they are fragrant.

2. Add the tomatoes, along with the peeled and cubed sweet potatoes. Cook for about 30 minutes, adding water if it seems to be drying out.

3. Divide the cauliflower into florets and add them to the pan with the coconut milk. Put the lid on and simmer for around 8 minutes, or until soft.

4. Meanwhile, gently toast the cashew nuts in a dry skillet.

5. Season with salt and pepper, then add the nuts just before serving

TIPS

o   Add spinach, cilantro, or peas for a little color.

o   Serve with rice and a spoonful of plain yogurt.

Mima has a tiny drop of Indian blood in her, which means she feels entitled to invent curries willy-nilly. This one has become a staple dinner at home in Dalston. *Henry*

Mima in Egypt, 2005

FRIENDS & FAMILY RECIPES

KERALAN FISH CURRY

This is a simple south Indian fish curry.

Feeds: 4
Preparation time: 10 minutes
Cooking time: 20 minutes
✓ WF DF GF

1 **fresh green chile**
1 teaspoon **canola oil**, to make the paste
1 teaspoon **ground coriander**
½ teaspoon **turmeric**
5 cloves of **garlic**
1 inch piece of **fresh ginger**
1 tablespoon **coconut oil** or **canola oil**
½ teaspoon **fenugreek seeds**
4 small **onions**
½ cup **coconut milk**
1 lb **mackerel fillets**
sea salt and freshly ground **black pepper**

1. Seed the chile, put it into a blender with the canola oil, coriander, turmeric, and peeled garlic and ginger, and process to form a paste.

2. Heat the coconut oil in a saucepan and sauté the paste and the fenugreek seeds.

3. Peel the onions, slice finely, and add them to the pan with the coconut milk and 1¼ cups of water. Season well with salt and pepper. Bring to a boil and keep it at a gentle boil until the sauce reduces, which should take about 5 minutes.

4. Cut the mackerel into 2 inch pieces and add to the curry. Simmer gently until the fish is cooked through, which should take between 5 and 8 minutes.

TIPS

o Best served with rice.

o You can use shrimp or white fish if mackerel is too strong for your taste.

o The mackerel should be very fresh, because it develops too strong a flavor if kept for too long in the refrigerator.

Honeymoon Vegetable Curry (above); Keralan Fish Curry (below)

HONEYMOON VEGETABLE CURRY

Not the most beautiful of curries, but a great staple for a simple healthy dinner (pictured on page 100).

Feeds: 4
Preparation time: 15 minutes
Cooking time: 20 minutes
✓ WF DF GF V

4 **zucchini**
2 **carrots**
2 **eggplants**
¼ of an **onion**
2 **fresh green chiles**
1 cup **coconut milk**
½ teaspoon **ground cumin**
¼ teaspoon **turmeric**
1 **lime**
sea salt and **freshly ground black pepper**

RECIPE TESTED BY MATILDA

1. Chop the zucchini into diagonal slices. Peel and chop the carrots into chunky batons and chop the eggplants into cubes. Peel and coarsely chop the onion, and seed the chiles.

2. Place the coconut milk, chiles, onion, and cumin into a food processor and process to a paste.

3. Dry-fry the turmeric in a saucepan for a minute, then add the vegetables and 1 cup of water. Bring to a boil, then reduce the heat and simmer for about 15 minutes, or until tender.

4. Add the coconut milk paste and cook gently for another 5 minutes.

5. Season, and squeeze with the juice of the lime before serving.

TIPS

o Serve on white basmati or other long-grain rice.

Mima and I went to Kerala, in southern India, for our honeymoon, largely because we knew the food would be really tasty. We were not disappointed. At the Coconut Lagoon, a swanky eco-hotel on a lake, the in-house entertainment included a tour of the hotel's composting system or lunchtime cooking lessons with the resident chef. We did both, and brought this recipe home as a souvenir (of the food, not the composter). *Henry*

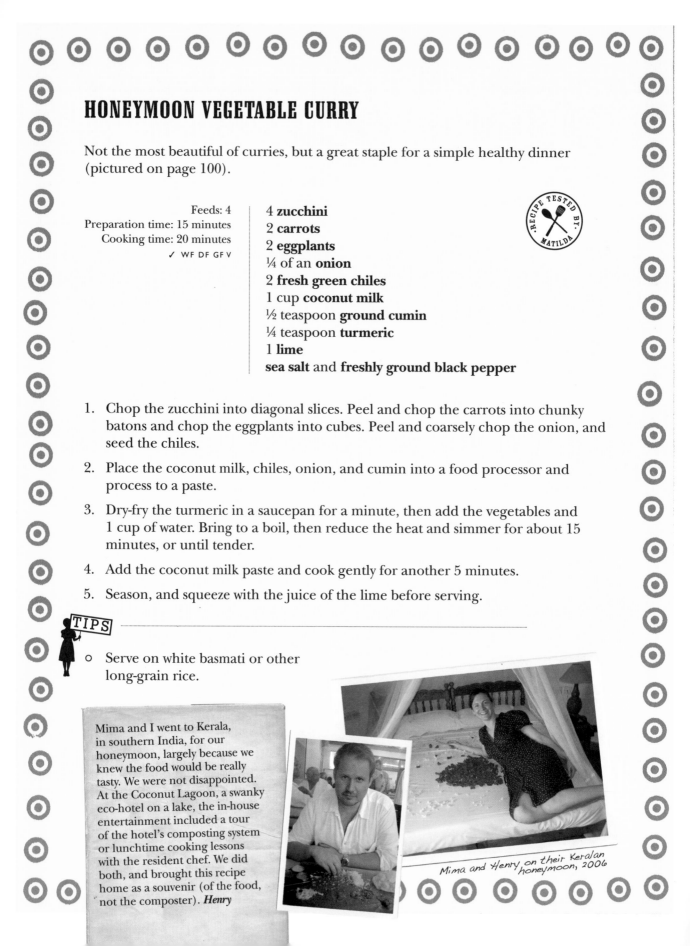

Mima and Henry on their Keralan honeymoon, 2006

SOUTH INDIAN PEPPER CHICKEN

The trick with this dish is to be bold with the black pepper—remember it is an ingredient, not a seasoning (pictured on page 104).

Feeds: 2
Preparation time: 15 minutes
Cooking time: 20–25 minutes
♥ ✓ WF DF GF

1 lb **chicken thighs**
1 tablespoon **olive oil**
4 cloves of **garlic**
1 inch piece of **fresh ginger**
1 **onion**
2 **tomatoes**
1 teaspoon **turmeric**
a small handful of **fresh cilantro leaves**
sea salt and plenty of **freshly ground black pepper**

About five years ago we traveled with our friend Gowri to Kerala and Tamil Nadu, where we were looked after by her family. Most of the best dishes in the south of India are vegetarian (worthy of a whole Leon book, maybe), but this was a chicken dish that satisfied our carnivorous cravings. Henry has recreated it for this book.
John and Katie

1. Cut each chicken thigh into 2 or 3 pieces with a heavy knife. Season with a lot of pepper and some salt, then add some more pepper.

2. Heat the oil in a saucepan and brown the chicken, turning it a few times to make sure the thighs are browned all over. Remove the chicken from the pan.

3. Peel and finely chop the garlic and ginger. Slice the onions. Cut the tomatoes into rough ½ inch dice.

4. Add the ginger, garlic, onions, and turmeric to the pan and sauté for a couple of minutes. Add the tomatoes and a couple of tablespoons of water. Cover, turn down the heat, and simmer for 2 minutes.

5. Put the chicken back into the pan, cover with a lid, and cook until tender. Season with salt and pepper, then stir in the chopped cilantro leaves.

TIPS

o   Goes very well with some rice and a good TV program.

Kate and Gowri in Kerala, 2005

Cruising on a houseboat, Kerala, 2005

SPICE FRIED FISH *with red onion*

This is a quick fish dish that works well as a side with a spread of vegetable dishes.

Feeds: 4
Preparation time: 5 minutes
Cooking time: 15 minutes
♥ ✓ DF

2 teaspoons **coriander seed**
2 teaspoons **cumin seed**
2 teaspoons **black peppercorns**
2 teaspoons **black mustard seed**
2 tablespoons **buckwheat** or **all-purpose flour**
a handful of crushed **cashew nuts**
2 **red onions**
⅛ cup **canola oil**
1 lb **sustainable white fish**
sea salt and **freshly ground black pepper**

1. Mix the coriander, cumin, peppercorns, and mustard seed with 2 teaspoons of sea salt and grind to a powder (best done in a clean coffee grinder). Put into a bowl and add the buckwheat flour. Check the seasoning. The flavor should be strong.

2. Put your widest skillet over high heat and toast the crushed cashew nuts. Remove them from the skillet and set aside.

3. Peel the onions and slice as finely as you can. Add them to the skillet with 2 tablespoons of the oil. Cook over high heat, stirring continually so that they brown and start to soften. Season, then remove the onions from the skillet.

4. Add the rest of the oil to the skillet. Cut the fish fillets into rough credit-card-size pieces, toss in the flour mix, and shallow-fry them until crisp and brown (about 2 minutes on each side). Unless you have a monster skillet you will need to do this in batches.

5. Put the fish on a serving plate and sprinkle with the onions and nuts.

TIPS

o Use any cheap sustainable white fish—coley, whiting, pollock and pouting all work well.

o If you don't have the individual spices, substitute 3 teaspoons of garam masala.

o Experiment with your own spice combinations. Add some chilli to the spice mix if you like it fiery.

o This works well with a little chopped fresh cilantro sprinkled on top.

o If you don't want to fry the onions, try just thinly slicing them and dressing them with lime juice and a touch of salt.

South Indian Pepper Chicken (above); Spice Fried Fish with Red Onion (below)

JOHN'S THAI CURRY

The green chicken curry has become the chicken tikka masala of the western Thai restaurant scene. You can replicate it in your own home very easily and quickly, thanks to the Thai curry pastes available. However, be sure to stay away from prepared sauces: they will leave you disappointed. Use only a high-quality paste and start from there.

Feeds: 4
Preparation time: 15 minutes
Cooking time: 15 minutes
✓ WF DF GF

4 **chicken thighs**
1 tablespoon **olive oil**
2–3 tablespoons **Thai curry paste**
1¾ cups of **coconut milk**
1 (8 oz) can of **bamboo shoots**
100g **Thai baby eggplants**
2 tablespoons **Thai fish sauce**
a few leaves of **fresh Thai sweet basil**
sea salt and **freshly ground black pepper**

1. Remove the meat from the chicken thighs and cut into thin strips.

2. Heat the olive oil in a large skillet, add the Thai curry paste, and stir the paste into the oil as you cook over hot heat for a minute.

3. Gradually add the coconut milk, followed by the chicken.

4. Drain and add the bamboo shoots, and the Thai baby eggplants, then simmer for 10 minutes.

5. Add the fish sauce, then taste and adjust the seasoning with salt and pepper, if you want to.

6. Sprinkle the curry with fresh sweet basil and serve.

 **TIPS**

I first tasted Green Chicken Curry not in Thailand but at college when a small Thai restaurant opened in the town. I thought it was one of the tastiest things I had ever eaten. Nowadays, it's a dish that has become a staple dish on most British "food service" restaurants and pubs. But many restaurants who are not authentically Thai seem to get it wrong and the sauces you can buy in supermarkets are no better. Having had the chance to visit Thailand a couple of times, I can confirm the view of many others that there are few better things than sitting on a Thai beach eating this dish, maybe with a Phad Thai, too. *John*

○ If you cannot find Thai sweet basil, use normal basil instead.

○ Serve with jasmine rice or even brown rice.

○ Get the right paste (try Asian grocery stores), and don't buy the sauces that come in jars.

○ The chicken will cook more quickly and taste much better if it is cut into thin strips instead of big chunks.

○ Add the coconut milk slowly, and stir as you do so to prevent the paste and the coconut milk from separating.

○ Thai baby eggplants are nothing like the eggplants we are used to. You can buy them in Asian grocery stores in jars. If you cannot find them, order some seeds online and grow your own, or add peas instead.

Corner Shop Classics

In most urban neighborhoods, the fourth emergency service is the corner shop or convenience store. Nestling between magazines and lottery tickets, you can generally find enough staple ingredients to rustle together a tasty meal, even at a modest store.

Here are some of our favorite 911 meals for when the cupboard is completely bare.

ULTIMATE CHEESE ON TOAST ✓ v

When done well, nothing can beat the bubbling crispy brown homeliness of this dish. Keep a good, seedy sliced bread in your freezer and toast it slice by slice.

This recipe is very hard to beat.

1. A good bread, toasted.

2. Butter, spread on the toast.

3. Dijon mustard, spread on top of the butter.

4. Fine slices of tomato, in one layer on top of the mustard.

5. Cheddar cheese (a good one if you have it), sliced into pieces the thickness of a hardback book cover and laid on top of the tomato, 2 slices deep.

6. A good fresh grind of black pepper.

7. Put under the broiler until melted and starting to bubble and brown.

8. Splash on some Worcestershire sauce.

9. Eat on its own or with baked beans.

Variations on a theme

○ **Cheese and Onion:** Grate the cheese and mix it with some finely sliced onion.

○ **Hot Horseradish:** Replace the Dijon mustard with some horseradish sauce.

○ **Cheese on Sea:** Slice a canned sardine in half and put it on top of the tomatoes before adding the cheese.

Hawk (left) and Tuzuk (aka Sahin and Suleyman) at Greenwood Road Costcutter, Henry's local convenience store

ULTIMATE MUSHROOMS ON TOAST ✓ ᵥ

A chef friend of ours once said that he believed the common button mushroom would be an expensive delicacy if it was rare. The way that it colors and deepens in flavor as it cooks is a wonder. Don't feel you need fancy mushrooms to make the ultimate mushrooms on toast.

1. A good bread, toasted.

2. Butter, spread on the toast.

3. A good pat of butter and a trickle of vegetable oil in a hot saucepan. The butter should foam.

4. A generous handful of sliced button mushrooms thrown into the pan with a tablespoon of finely sliced onion. Don't move them around too much. Toss every 30 seconds or so, but give them time to turn golden. Season.

5. Finely chopped garlic and fresh parsley thrown in for the last 30 seconds.

6. A squeeze of lemon juice and onto the toast.

Variations on a theme

○ **Luxury:** Instead of lemon juice add a splash of white wine at the end. When this has bubbled off, add a tablespoon of heavy cream and bubble for 20 seconds before offloading onto the toast.

○ **Meaty:** Before you cook the mushrooms, sauté some prosciutto in the pan until it turns crispy. Stick it on top like a shark's fin.

○ **Toast on Mushrooms on Toast:** This was an accident we discovered while photographing the pictures for this book. Nothing in the world tastes better. Sauté some bread crumbs with garlic and seasoning until they are crispy. Make the Ultimate Mushrooms on Toast. Sprinkle the garlic bread crumbs on top for extra crunch.

BEAN SALAD *with quick pickled onions*

Simple, fresh, and healthy—pickling the onions like this sweetens them and takes away the raw onion flavor.

Feeds: 4
Preparation time: 15 minutes
Cooking time: 0 minutes
♥ ✓ WF DF GF V

1 clove of **garlic**
1 **lemon**
a large handful of chopped **fresh flat-leaf parsley**
1 large **red onion**
2 medium **vine-ripened tomatoes**
2 tablespoons **extra virgin olive oil**
2 (15 oz) cans of **cannellini beans**
sea salt and **freshly ground black pepper**

1. Peel the garlic. On the finest holes of your grater, grate the garlic and lemon zest and mix it in a small bowl with the chopped parsley.

2. Peel the red onion and slice as finely as you can. Put the slices into a bowl with a few pinches of sea salt and the lemon juice. Let stand for 5 minutes.

3. Chop the tomatoes into coarse chunks. Season with salt and add them to the onions, along with the olive oil and the drained beans. Toss really well to combine the flavors. Season.

4. Let the salad sit until you get a nice pooling of tomato juice at the bottom—the magic juice. This will take around 5–10 minutes.

5. When ready to eat, stir in the parsley, lemon, and garlic mixture, then serve.

TIPS

o Serve with sourdough toast for a simple dinner.

o Add toasted seeds or almonds.

o Substitute other fresh green herbs for the parsley.

o There are three things that raise this dish above the ordinary: the pickled onions; letting it sit so the juices steep; and the raw parsley, lemon, and garlic mixture at the end. You can try all kinds of combinations of different beans and vegetables (raw, grated zucchini are a great addition, as is grated carrot).

Bean Salad with Quick Pickled Onions (above); Quick Bean & Lettuce Stew (below)

QUICK BEAN & LETTUCE STEW

For days when you have no time, but want something that's properly nourishing (pictured on page 112).

Feeds: 4
Preparation time: 5 minutes
Cooking time: 15 minutes
♥ ✓ WF DF GF

6 slices of **bacon**
2 cloves of **garlic**
¼ cup **olive oil**
¼ teaspoon **fennel seeds**
1 (14½ oz) can of **diced tomatoes**
1 cup **chicken stock**
1 (15 oz) can of **cannellini beans**
¼ head of romaine **lettuce**
sea salt and **freshly ground black pepper**

1. Chop the bacon and garlic. Heat the olive oil in a saucepan and add the bacon. Cook for a few minutes, then add the chopped garlic and fennel seeds.

2. Pour in the canned tomatoes and cook over high heat for 5 minutes.

3. Add the stock and the drained beans, and cook for another 5 minutes.

4. Season well, add the chopped lettuce, and let it wilt before serving.

5. Drizzle with olive oil and sprinkle with plenty of black pepper.

TIPS

○ This works with all kinds of beans.

○ If you want to make it a vegetarian dish, replace the bacon with a few chopped ripe black olives.

HATTIE'S SWEET ONION FRITTATA

This is a very economical and cheap meal to have with salad and a chunk of bread (pictured on page 116).

Feeds: 4
Preparation time: 15 minutes
Cooking time: 30 minutes
✓ WF GF V

7 **onions** (about 1¾ lb)
a handful of **fresh flat-leaf parsley**
3½ tablespoons **butter**
8 extra-large **eggs**
sea salt and **freshly ground black pepper**

1. Peel the onions and slice into thin semicircles. Coarsely chop the parsley. Melt the butter in a large skillet and add the onions. Cook over gentle heat, covered with a lid if you have one, for 25 minutes, or until the onions are soft and sweet. Meanwhile, preheat the broiler to medium heat.

2. Crack the eggs into a bowl and mix well, seasoning with salt and pepper.

3. Add the onion mixture to the eggs, mix well and add the chopped parsley. Return the mixture to the skillet that the onions were cooking in, or a smaller one if the original is wide and will make the frittata too shallow.

4. Very gently cook the frittata on the stove, watching carefully to avoid letting it burn on the bottom. When you think it's cooked through, apart from the top, which will still be runny, place it under the broiler to finish off the top.

5. Let cool to lukewarm, and serve with a green salad.

TIPS

○ Grated Parmesan is a good addition to the egg mixture. You can mix any leftover vegetables with the onions, too. Peas and bell peppers go well, as do cold potatoes and any old ends of cheese that you might want to use up.

○ To make this into a quiche or tart, line a 10 inch flan pan with puff pastry or rolled dough pie crust (if using rolled dough, you will need to bake it for 15 minutes in the preheated oven first). Add the onion filling and bake it in the oven at 350°F for 25–30 minutes, or until golden and firm.

Hattie picnicking, 1979

PRIORITY
This easy and economical dish has been a staple in our household for years. It is very easy, and every time we make it we find ourselves adding new things to it. We even made vast amounts for our wedding party and they went down well.
Hattie

FRIENDS & FAMILY RECIPES

RECIPE TESTED BY JACKIE & AMY

JOHN DERHAM'S STUFFED PEPPERS

Allow one whole tomato per half of red bell pepper.

Feeds: 4 (as a side)
Preparation time: 10 minutes
Cooking time: 30 minutes

♥ ✓ WF DF GF

RECIPE TESTED BY JANE

2 large **red bell peppers**
4 **tomatoes**
4 cloves of **garlic**
2 tablespoons **extra virgin olive oil**
8 **anchovy fillets**
sea salt and **freshly ground black pepper**

John Derham (Katie's Dad) and John's brother Tony, 1958

FRIENDS & FAMILY RECIPES

1. Preheat the oven to 475°F.

2. Halve and seed the bell peppers.

3. Remove the cores from the tomatoes and pour over boiling water, let stand for 2 minutes, then drain and plunge into cold water. When cool, peel off the skins and put 1 tomato into each bell pepper half.

4. Crush the garlic and spread under and over the tomatoes as they sit in the peppers. Drizzle with olive oil and season with salt and pepper.

5. Lay 2 anchovy fillets over each tomato, and bake in the oven for 30 minutes, turning the oven temperature down to 400°F after the first 10 minutes.

This classic French recipe was first brought to Great Britain by Elizabeth David in her book *Italian Food*. So simple, yet so good. This is Katie's dad John's take on it. Ripe in-season bell peppers are essential. When Katie and I were first going out, we would spend weekends at her mom and dad's house in Wilmslow and John would, with a glass of wine always somewhere close by, make great dinners for the family. This dish is one John often includes in his repertoire, making it while listening to Cuban music in high fidelity.
John

JOHN'S FRIED EGGPLANTS

RECIPE TESTED BY LISA

Feeds: 4
Preparation time: 5 minutes
Cooking time: 20 minutes

♥ ✓ WF DF GF V

3 small **eggplants**
3 cloves of **garlic**
¼ cup **extra virgin olive oil**
½ cup **light olive oil** or **vegetable oil**
juice of ½ a **lemon**
sea salt and **freshly ground black pepper**

1. Cut the tops off the eggplants and slice each one lengthwise into ¼-inch thick slices. Place on a baking sheet and sprinkle liberally with salt.

2. Let stand for 5 minutes to draw the moisture out, then rinse the slices under clold running water and dry thoroughly with paper towels.

3. Peel and finely mince or grate the garlic and put into a clean bowl with the extra virgin olive oil and some pepper.

4. Put your largest skillet over medium heat, and sauté the eggplants in batches in the light olive oil, until golden brown and soft, turning them over halfway through.

5. When the eggplants are cooked, place them on a plate and dress with the garlic oil and a squeeze of lemon juice.

Katie and I made this dish many times just after we got married in 1999, so we tend to associate it with TV dinners in our small apartment in Paddington, probably watching *Sex and the City* or some other late-Nineties U.S. show. We used to eat it with the Stuffed Peppers and together these form the basis of a great flavorful vegetable-based dinner. Leftovers of both can be put into a lunch-bag for the next day.
John

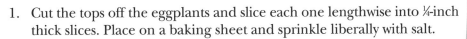
Clockwise from left: John's Fried Eggplants; Hattie's Sweet Onion Frittata; John Derham's Stuffed Peppers

TOM'S RED PESTO SURPRISE

Ideal comfort food, and perfect for curing a lingering hangover. No one has quite worked out what the surprise is yet.

Feeds: 4
Preparation time: 5 minutes
Cooking time: 20 minutes
DF

5 cloves of **garlic**
2 **onions**
8 oz **smoked bacon**
3 tablespoons **olive oil**
2⅓ cups **frozen peas**
1 lb **penne**
3–4 tablespoons good **red pesto**

1. Put a saucepan of salted water on to boil. Peel and finely chop the garlic and onions, and cut the bacon into small chunks.

2. Sauté the garlic and onions in the olive oil in a large, heavy skillet for 5 minutes. Add the chopped bacon and cook for another 3 minutes. Add the peas and stir well, coating them well with oil, then cook for around 10 minutes over slow heat.

3. While the sauce is simmering, cook your pasta according to the directions on the package, and drain, retaining 1 tablespoon of the cooking water. Put the pasta back into the pan with the reserved water to keep it moist.

4. When the peas are cooked and you are ready to eat, stir in the pesto. Add the pasta and stir well. Serve immediately.

TIPS

The key is not to be mean with your pesto. If you feel it needs more, add more.

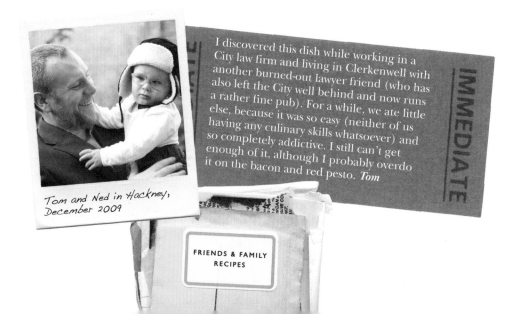

Tom and Ned in Hackney, December 2009

I discovered this dish while working in a City law firm and living in Clerkenwell with another burned-out lawyer friend (who has also left the City well behind and now runs a rather fine pub). For a while, we ate little else, because it was so easy (neither of us having any culinary skills whatsoever) and so completely addictive. I still can't get enough of it, although I probably overdo it on the bacon and red pesto. *Tom*

IMMEDIATE

FRIENDS & FAMILY RECIPES

THE FRIDGE IS BARE.

YOU FORGOT TO STOP OFF AT THE CORNER SHOP ON YOUR WAY HOME.

YOU DON'T HAVE THE CASH FOR A DELIVERY.

THESE ARE THE RECIPES THAT WILL HELP YOU LIVE TO FIGHT ANOTHER DAY.

THESE ARE OUR STORE CUPBOARD STAPLES.

PASTA WITH PEAS

Even in the depths of a nuclear winter, you could probably rustle together the ingredients for this dish—unsophisticated but cozy, perfect for a TV dinner.

Feeds: 4
Preparation time: 5 minutes
Cooking time: 15 minutes
♥

2 **onions**
3 cloves of **garlic**
2 **leeks**
¼ cup **olive oil**
a thumb-size piece of **butter**
1 lb **penne**
1⅓ cups **frozen peas**
juice of 1 **lemon**
Parmesan cheese to taste
sea salt and **freshly ground black pepper**

1. Peel and coarsely chop the onions and garlic. Trim and slice the leeks thinly.

2. Heat the oil and butter in a saucepan over medium heat. Add the onions and soften for a few minutes.

3. Add the leeks and garlic, stir, and let cook over very low heat with the lid on. Check and stir every so often to make sure the leeks aren't browning. You may need to add a few drops of water (or white wine, if you have some on hand).

4. Meanwhile, put the pasta on to boil. Two minutes before it will be ready, stir the peas and lemon juice into the leek and onion mixture and continue to cook over medium heat until the peas are just cooked through. Season with salt and pepper.

5. Drain the pasta, return it to the pan, stir in the vegetables, and serve in bowls, topped with generous handfuls of Parmesan.

 TIPS

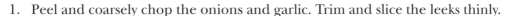

o If you don't have any leeks, mushrooms are wonderful. Sliced red bell peppers are not bad either.

Left: Pasta with Peas; Right: Spaghetti Puttanesca

SPAGHETTI PUTTANESCA

Take all the greatest-tasting pantry ingredients, turn them into a spaghetti sauce, and this is what you get (pictured on page 120).

Feeds: 4
Preparation time: 5 minutes
Cooking time: 25 minutes
♥ DF

2 cloves of **garlic**
1 (2 oz) can of **anchovies**
1 tablespoon **capers**
¼ cup **extra virgin olive oil**
1 **dried chile** or 1 teaspoon **chile powder**
1 teaspoon **dried oregano**
2 small **white onions**
1 cup drained **pitted ripe black olives**
1 (14½ oz) can of **diced tomatoes**
1 lb dried **spaghetti**
sea salt and **freshly ground black pepper**

1. Fill a saucepan with salted water and bring it to a boil.

2. Peel and finely chop the garlic, and finely chop the anchovies and capers. Heat the oil in a skillet over medium heat, and add the chopped ingredients. Crumble in the dried chile and oregano, and let brown gently.

3. Peel and finely chop the onions and add to the skillet with the olives. Coat everything well and pour in the tomatoes together with ½ cup of water. Increase the heat so that the sauce is bubbling.

4. Stir regularly and cook until the tomatoes have become a darker color.

5. Cook your spaghetti as per the package directions, then drain but retain a few tablespoons of water to keep the pasta loose. Transfer the pasta into the sauce and mix slowly and well, using 2 forks. Top with black pepper and Parmesan if you derire, and serve.

 TIPS

○ Add a chopped fresh chile for extra fire.

○ Clearly this will go well with other pastas besides spaghetti.

○ A little chopped parsley added at the end freshens it up nicely.

FULL OF
SUN

TUSCAN BEANS *with sage*

A vinegary bean dish, great as a side or as a summer salad (pictured on page 124).

Feeds: 4
Preparation time: 5 minutes
Cooking time: 20 minutes
♥ ✓ WF DF GF

2 cloves of **garlic**
½ an **onion**
3 tablespoons **olive oil**
4 **anchovy** fillets
1 cup **fresh sage**
3 tablespoons **red wine vinegar**
1 (15 oz) can of **cranberry beans**
sea salt and **freshly ground black pepper**

1. Peel the garlic, crush it, and coarsely chop. Peel the onion and coarsely slice. Sauté both gently in the olive oil.

2. Coarsely chop the anchovies and sage, add to the saucepan with the vinegar and ½ cup of water, and simmer gently for 10 minutes.

3. Drain the beans, add them to the pan, and cook for another 10 minutes. Season.

TIPS

○ To make this a little more indulgent and creamy, add a pat of butter just before serving.

○ Add chopped fresh parsley at the end for some color.

This dish was inspired by a recipe in *Beaneaters & Bread Soup* by Lori de Mori and Jason Lowe. Jason takes the photographs for our restaurant menu boards and is a force of nature, with wild red hair and an elemental passion for food. The original *fabioli al fiasco*—literally "beans in a flask"—is made in a glass wine flask stopped with a wad of flax. The whole thing is left in the embers of a fire overnight. Not a particularly safe procedure, and one which Jason surmises might have led to our current usage of the word "fiasco."
Henry

FRIENDS & FAMILY RECIPES

The original " fabioli al fiasco"—beans in a flask.
Photograph by Jason Lowe.

MIMA'S GREEK-ISH LIMA BEANS

Cheap, cheesy, and healthy—this dish will tide you over when the refrigerator is completely bare.

Feeds: 4
Preparation time: 5 minutes
Cooking time: 40 minutes
✓ WF GF V

2 tablespoons **olive oil**
2 **red onions**
4 cloves of **garlic**
2 level teaspoons **fennel seeds**
2 teaspoons **dried oregano**
2 (28 oz) can of **diced tomatoes**
2 heaping teaspoons **tomato paste**
3 (15 oz) cans of **lima beans**
8 oz **feta cheese**
sea salt and **freshly ground black pepper**

1. Heat the oil in a large saucepan. Peel and chop the onions and sauté gently for a couple of minutes. Peel and chop the garlic, and add it to the pan with the fennel seeds and oregano. Cook over low heat, stirring occasionally, until the mixture looks unctuous and soft.

2. Add the canned tomatoes and tomato paste, and let simmer for 20 minutes. Add the drained beans and continue to simmer for another 10 minutes. Season.

3. Crumble most of the feta into the stew, stir well, then divide among bowls and garnish with a final crumble of feta.

 TIPS

○ For an extra hit of protein, fry or poach an egg and slap it on top.

Mima in Oxford, 1978

I made this up after returning home from a vacation in Greece, craving some permutation of tomato sauce with feta cheese. It is totally inauthentic, but I love it.
Mima

FRIENDS & FAMILY RECIPES

Mima's Greek-ish Lima beans (above)

Tuscan Beans with Sage (below)

Anchovies and cream

Melt the anchovies in a little oil until they break up, then mix in the cream and plenty of pepper

Butter, pepper, and herbs

Chop the herbs finely and turn everything into the hot pasta

Garlic bread crumbs

Sauté the bread crumbs in some olive oil with finely chopped garlic, salt, and pepper

Blue cheese

Simply crumble over the hot pasta with a little butter and pepper

Pecans, parsley, basil, and chile

Warm some olive oil gently in a saucepan. Chop everything finely, drop into the olive oil, stir briefly, then turn into the pasta

Almonds and garlic

Finely chop the garlic and melt gently in some butter. Turn through pasta. Season. Add the almonds on top.

CAPER & ANCHOVY MIRACLE SAUCE

There is almost nothing in this world of ours that won't be improved through the addition of this pantry classic.

Use it to:

1 Spoon over cooked green vegetables or boiled potatoes.

2 Drizzle over grilled, broiled, or poached meat and fish.

3 Dress thin slices of roasted pumpkin or butternut squash.

4 Top mashed hard-boiled eggs on toast.

5 Dress a tomato and mozzarella salad.

6 And much, much more.

Makes: 1 cup
Preparation time: 4 minutes
Cooking time: 0 minutes
✓ WF DF GF

8 **anchovy fillets**
1 cup **extra virgin olive oil**
3 tablespoons **capers**
1 tablespoon fresh **lemon juice**
a large handful of chopped **fresh flat-leaf parsley**
freshly ground black pepper

1. Finely chop the anchovies and put them into a saucepan over medium heat with half the oil. They will dissolve (this will take about 3 minutes). Take them off the heat.

2. Finely chop the capers and add them to the pan with the rest of the olive oil and the lemon juice. Stir.

3. Season with pepper (you shouldn't need any salt) and add the chopped parsley.

 TIPS

○ If you have no lemon juice, you can use white wine vinegar.

○ If you want to add a little punch, finely chop 2 cloves of garlic and add them to the pan halfway through heating the anchovies.

○ The trick of dissolving anchovies like this also works as a good base for other savory or cream sauces.

LEON

RECIPE TESTED BY OLI & PETA

SUMMER SPEED

Summer is too hot to spend time sweating in the kitchen—and if it isn't too hot, it's too short.

So whether you like to spend these precious hours clocking up laps at the swimming pool, freaking out at a festival, or simply sinking into a deckchair with a good book, these recipes are designed to give you the time to do it.

BARBECUES

A magic word. Like Christmas. Or rebate.

A barbecue is a momentary holiday. If you are throwing one, you really want to be drinking, relaxing, and talking—not sweating over the coals. So it's a good idea to consider our friend Richard's advice: "the main thing is to keep the main thing the main thing." Cook one thing—whether it is a butterflied leg of lamb, a chicken, or a couple of squid— and serve it with a salad you made earlier. That way you should have plenty of time to sit back and enjoy your day.

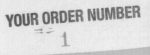

Mitch catching his first mackerel in Portmelon, Cornwall, 1974

MITCH'S BARBECUED SQUID
with chile & peppers

Smoky marinated squid, very sweet and very summery.

Feeds: 4
Preparation time: 5 minutes
Cooking time: 10 minutes
♥ ✓ WF DF GF

1 **red bell epper**
1 **fresh red chile**
1 teaspoon **dried red pepper flakes**
2 **bay leaves**
2 cloves of **garlic**
3 tablespoons **extra virgin olive oil**
1 teaspoon **coriander seeds**
2 **whole squid**, skins off, cleaned inside, tentacles left on—about 8 oz each
sea salt and **freshly ground black pepper**

This is an adaptation of a dish I first ate in a small but world-class restaurant in Dartmouth, Devon, called the Seahorse. The squid had been freshly plucked that day from the bay that was visible from the window. If you ever get the chance, I urge you to go there. The chef-proprietor, Mitch Tonks, is a master. If you can't make the trip, this recipe isn't a bad alternative. *Henry*

YOUR ORDER NUMBER
1

1. Light your grill with plenty of good lumpwood charcoal.

2. Put all the ingredients, except the squid, into a food processor and blend until smooth.

3. Pour into a bowl and add the squid, mixing to make sure that it is all covered by the marinade. Let the squid marinate for as long as you like.

4. When the barbecue coals are white and well burned down, put the squid on the grill and cook for around 5–8 minutes, turning once. Baste it with extra liquid as you cook it.

5. If you have any leftover marinade, pour it into a saucepan and bring to a boil, and serve it as a sauce.

TIPS

o   You can cut chunks off the squid, or slice it into rings, and eat it with a salad and bread.

o   Mitch blackens the bell peppers and removes their skins prior to cooking, which gives them an extra smoky flavor.

o   Coat the marinated squid in bread crumbs for crunch.

Mitch's Barbecued Squid (left); Butterflied Leg of Lamb with Mint Sauce

FRIENDS & FAMILY RECIPES

BUTTERFLIED LEG OF LAMB *with mint sauce*

If we could only barbecue one dish, this would be it. It is incredibly simple and surprisingly good (pictured on page 132).

For the Lamb

Feeds: 6–8
Preparation time: 10 minutes
Cooking time: 25–30 minutes
✓ WF DF GF

1 **leg of lamb** (about 3–3¼ lb), butterflied
(ask your butcher to do this and get him to trim the fat—
it's tasty but leads to unnecessary flare-ups on the grill)
sea salt and **freshly ground black pepper**

1. Light the grill. The heat of the grill is critical. Use a lot of good charcoal—lumpwood if possible—and wait until it has died down to lovely soft white embers. If you have good depth to the charcoal, you will be able to cook on it for over an hour.

2. Fill a cup with water. Season the meat well with salt and pepper. Do not rub it with oil—it just drips into the grill, causing flames and burning the meat. (If you have marinated the meat beforehand, pat the oil off.)

3. Put the meat on the grill and turn it every 5 minutes or so for 25–30 minutes. If it flares up, hurl on water from your cup.

4. Take the meat off and let it rest for up to 30 minutes.

5. Cut it across in chunks.

For the Mint Sauce

2 large handfuls of **fresh mint leaves**
2 tablespoons **honey**
½ cup **white wine vinegar**
sea salt

1. Wash the mint and chop it as finely as you can.

2. Put the mint into a small serving bowl and add the honey.

3. Stir it well, then add the vinegar. Season.

TIPS

○ Take your lamb out of the refrigerator an hour or so before cooking. It leads to more even cooking and makes it less likely that you will end up with something charred on the outside and raw on the inside.

○ This is a perfect piece of meat to marinade. You can do this well in advance. Put the meat into a large bowl with plenty of olive oil, chopped rosemary, garlic, and lemon zest.

○ You can use sugar or fructose in place of honey in the mint sauce.

○ We love mint sauce sharp, to cut through the fatty lamb. If it is too sharp for you, add more honey.

Liza, Sadie, Kate, and Binny, Devon 1979

THE EMPEROR OF THE BARBECUE: PORTERHOUSE STEAK
with Pierre's garlic potatoes & garlicky aioli WF GF DF

You will need to ask your butcher to prepare the Porterhouse steaks for you. Eat them with a green salad and a good bottle of red. The recipes that follow are in the order in which you need to cook them (all pictured on the following page).

Feeds: 4–6

The Potatoes

Preparation time: 5 minutes
Cooking time: 30 minutes

⅓ cup **olive oil**
1½ lb **new potatoes**
a large bunch of **fresh rosemary**
5 cloves of **garlic**
sea salt and **freshly ground black pepper**

1. Preheat the oven to 400°F. Light your grill with plenty of good lumpwood charcoal.

2. Pour the oil into a large roasting pan and put it into the oven to heat up for 5 minutes while you prepare the potatoes.

3. Halve the potatoes. Coarsely chop the rosemary and toss with the potatoes and the unpeeled garlic cloves. Season. Add them to the roasting pan of sizzling hot oil. Return the pan to the oven and roast for 20–25 minutes, until golden brown.

The Steak

Preparation time: 5 minutes
Cooking time: 10 minutes

2 **Porterhouse steaks**
Dijon mustard
sea salt and **freshly ground black pepper**

1. Smear your steaks liberally with Dijon mustard, salt, and pepper.

2. When the charcoal is white, well burned down, and not too hot, put the steaks on for about 5 minutes on each side (depending on how rare you like them).

3. Let the meat rest, covered in aluminum foil, for 5–10 minutes before serving, while you get the potatoes out of the oven and make the aioli.

The Aioli

Preparation time: 5 minutes
Cooking time: 0 minutes

3 cloves of **garlic**
3 **egg yolks**
1 level tablespoon **Dijon mustard**
⅔ cup **vegetable oil**
a squeeze of **lemon juice**
sea salt and **freshly ground black pepper**

1. Peel and coarsely chop the garlic and place in a food processor with the egg yolks, mustard, salt, and pepper.

2. Process together, then slowly drizzle in the oil while the processor is still running.

3. Check the seasoning and add a squeeze of lemon juice.

 TIPS

o It is critical that the grill is not too hot, otherwise you will produce raw steak with a charcoal crust.

o You can use T-bone steaks, which are the same cut but from farther down the animal so that you get less tenderloin.

o Thyme, marjoram, or oregano will work just as well with the potatoes if you don't like rosemary. For a warmer, smoky taste, you could use paprika instead of herbs.

o This is also a great way to cook quick roasted potatoes for a Sunday lunch.

o The aioli can be served with any grilled meat or fish, or simply for dipping a crust of bread into.

FRIENDS & FAMIL RECIPES

·RECIPE TESTED BY·
PIERRE

We ate this on a hot summer's day in our yard when a generous guest turned up with two huge slabs of meat. A Porterhouse steak is in fact two-in-one: a tenderloin steak and a top loin steak still joined together by the T-bone. We lit the grill and Pierre threw together some aioli and potatoes. The tenderloin on one side was sweet and buttery and the top loin on the other was rampant and gamey with age. Expensive but a great once-in-a-summer treat. *Henry*

BUTTERFLIED CHICKEN *with eggplants & tomatoes*

An elegant way to cook chicken on the grill without having to juggle loads of charring drummers.

Feeds: 4
Preparation time: 10 minutes
Cooking time: 40 minutes
✓ WF DF GF

1 medium **chicken** (about 2¼–3¼ lb)
4 sprigs of **fresh thyme**
juice of ½ **lemon**
1 large **eggplant**
2 tablespoons **extra virgin olive oil**
4 **tomatoes**
sea salt and **freshly ground black pepper**

1. First, light the grill. The heat of the grill is critical. Use a lot of good charcoal—lumpwood if possible—and wait until it has died down to lovely soft white embers. If you have good depth to the charcoal you will be able to cook on it for over an hour.

2. Butterfly the chicken (see opposite).

3. Finely chop the thyme. Rub the chicken with salt, pepper, and half the thyme, then squeeze the lemon juice over it. You can use oil, but this increases the risk of charring.

4. Cut the ends off the eggplant and slice lengthwise into ½ inch pieces. Toss in a bowl with the olive oil and the rest of the thyme. Cut the tomatoes in half and season the cut sides.

5. When the grill is ready, place the chicken on the grate, skin side down. Turn it every 5 minutes. Watch out for flaming—if the flames flare up, douse them with a good splash of water. It will take about 40 minutes to cook.

6. While you are cooking the chicken, cook the tomatoes and eggplant, in batches, alongside it. The eggplant will take about 2 minutes on each side. The tomatoes will take about 4 minutes on each side.

TIPS

○ Serve with Green Sauce (page 141).

○ If you don't want to butterfly your chicken yourself, ask your butcher to do it for you.

○ For extra show, you can squeeze a stuffing under the skin of the bird prior to cooking. Simple combinations work well. Think garlic and tarragon, fried mushrooms and thyme, or parsley and cream cheese. For the more adventurous, lime pickle processed with butter in the food processor is terrific, as is grated zucchini with Parmesan.

○ You can use the butterflying technique to reduce the time it takes to cook a roasted chicken. A butterflied chicken will roast in a 400°F oven in only 30 minutes.

JOY OF BUTTERFLYING

1. Put the bird on a board breast side down. Cut with the shears or a large knife one side of the backbone (classically, at this stage you would cut down the other side as well and entirely remove the backbone, but we think this isn't necessary).

2. Pull the legs apart. Put the bird cavity side down and push the whole thing flat. (Again, traditionally, you would remove the breastbone from inside the cavity. But this is not necessary either.)

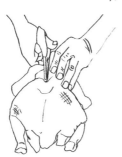

CHIMICHURRI SAUCE

An Argentinian sauce that comes to life when it hits hot meat.

Feeds: 4 (makes about 1¼ cups)
Preparation time: 10 minutes
Cooking time: 0 minutes
♥ ✓ WF DF GF V

a large handful of **fresh flat-leaf parsley**
2 cloves of **garlic**
1 tablespoon **smoked sweet paprika**
1 tablespoon **dried oregano** or **thyme**
1 tablespoon **cayenne pepper**
⅔ cup **extra virgin olive oil**
⅓ cup **red wine vinegar**
sea salt and **freshly ground black pepper**

1. Wash the parsley and shake dry. Peel the garlic.

2. Put all the ingredients into a blender and process until smooth.

3. Season.

TIPS

○ Traditionally served with beef, but it works well with lamb, too. It also works with fish that will stand up to it—for example, barbecued monkfish or cod.

○ Next time you are invited to a grill, take a big container of this along as well as your chops. You will be very popular.

○ Also good heated briefly in a saucepan and poured over boiled vegetables for a healthy dinner.

GREEN SAUCE

A fresh, vibrant sauce that goes with almost anything.

Feeds: 4 (makes about 1⅛ cups)
Preparation time: 10 minutes
Cooking time: 0 minutes
♥ ✓ WF DF GF

a large handful of **fresh mint**
a large handful of **fresh flat-leaf parsley**
a large handful of **fresh cilantro**
1 tablespoon **capers**
2 teaspoons **Dijon mustard**
4 **anchovy fillets**
1 cup **extra virgin olive oil**
juice of ½ a **lemon**
sea salt and **freshly ground black pepper**

1. Put all the ingredients into a blender and process until smooth. It should be runny but substantial.

2. Transfer to a sealable jar and refrigerate.

TIPS

○ Serve with any simply barbecued, grilled or roasted meat or fish—it is that versatile.

○ Spoon over vegetables for a simple dinner.

○ You can omit the anchovies if you need to—but they do give a rich depth of flavor.

○ Use any green herbs you have on hand—basil and tarragon both work well, too.

INDIAN BARBECUE SAUCE

An easy grill sauce that can double as a marinade.

Feeds: 4 (makes about 1¼ cups)
Preparation time: 5 minutes
Cooking time: 0 minutes
♥ ✓ WF GF V

1 cup **plain yogurt**
3 teaspoons good **tikka masala paste**
½ a **lemon**
a large handful of **fresh coriander**

1. Put the yogurt into a bowl and stir in the tikka masala paste.

2. Add lemon juice and chopped coriander to taste.

TIPS

○ Great with lamb, chicken, or beef.

○ Dip cooked meat into this sauce, or use it to marinate meat before putting it on the grill.

FULL OF
SUN

STUFFED PICNIC BREAD LOAF

A great picnic dish—your imagination is the only thing limiting what can go inside it.

Feeds: 8
Preparation time: 10 minutes
Cooking time: 0 minutes

1 medium **round, crusty bread loaf**
½ jar of **pesto**
1–1¼ cups **cream cheese**
4–8 oz **salami**
1 large **red bell pepper**
½ cup **sun-dried tomatoes**
4 oz **prosciutto ham**
large handful of **fresh spinach leaves**
sea salt and **freshly ground black pepper**

1. Cut the top off the loaf and scrape out the bread inside, leaving the crusty shell. Reserve the top.

2. Spread the inside of the loaf with a thin layer of pesto.

3. Start layering up the loaf with cream cheese, salami slices, thin slices of red bell pepper, tomatoes, prosciutto and spinach, sprinkling with salt and pepper as you work, and repeating the layers until the loaf is full. Cover with plastic wrap and put something heavy on top to weigh it down.

4. Let stand in the refrigerator for at least 4 hours.

5. Put the top back on and either serve cold or put into a hot oven for 5 minutes to crisp it up—wrap it in aluminum foil. To serve, slice like a cake.

 TIPS

- You can make this 12 hours before you leave for your picnic.

- Just about anything can be layered in the loaf:

- **Veggie option:** with roasted butternut squash, chargrilled zucchini, roasted red peppers, roasted mushrooms, spinach leaves, pesto, and Parmesan shavings.

- **Fish option:** with smoked salmon, arugula leaves, sun-dried tomatoes, lettuce, lemon juice, black pepper, crème fraîche.

- **Meat option:** with chicken, mayonnaise, lettuce, tomatoes and bacon.

- You can use all the prepared antipasti from a delicatessen—artichoke hearts in oil, chargrilled peppers and zucchini, marinated mushrooms, anchovies, etc. The world is your oyster.

Nat, Daisy, Eleanor, Natasha, Clemmie, Mabel, Wilf, George & Arthur, 2009

I saw something similar to this recipe in an Australian housekeeping magazine years ago. We now try and spend as much time in north Norfolk (my old stomping ground), as possible and often take our leaky little day boat out at Brancaster. Fried eggs and bacon cooked on the Calor gas for breakfast and then the cob loaf for lunch, which I made the night before. Magical! *Apple*

A comely collection of colorful coolers

CUCUMBER COOLER

This might just be the most beautiful-looking drink in the world, and it's refreshing, too.

Makes 8¾ cups (before ice)
♥ ✓ WF DF GF V

1 **cucumber**
1 **lime**
6½ cups **cold water**

1. Peel the cucumber, discarding the peel. Then, still using the peeler, keep peeling the flesh into long ribbons, turning it as you work. Drop the cucumber ribbons straight into your favorite pitcher, and keep making more until you get to the seeds.

2. Squeeze in the juice of the lime, and add the water and plenty of ice.

MELON FIZZ

Makes 6 cups
♥ ✓ WF DF GF V

1 ripe **cantaloupe melon**
juice of 2 **limes**
4 cups **cold sparkling water**

1. Peel the melon and remove the seeds. Chop the flesh and blend it in a food processor with the juice of 1 lime.

2. Pour through a fine strainer into a wide-necked pitcher or bowl, squeezing as much of the juice through as you can.

3. Fill up with sparkling water and serve.

SPARKLING STRAWBERRY COOLER

Makes 6 cups
♥ ✓ WF DF GF V

1 pint **strawberries**
6 **fresh mint leaves**
juice of **1 lemon**
2 tablespoons **honey**
4 cups **cold sparkling water**

1. Process everything except the water in a blender.

2. Add ice to the blender if you desire.

3. Transfer to a pitcher, and mix in the sparkling water, and serve.

From left: Sparkling Strawberry Cooler; Cucumber Cooler; Melon Fizz

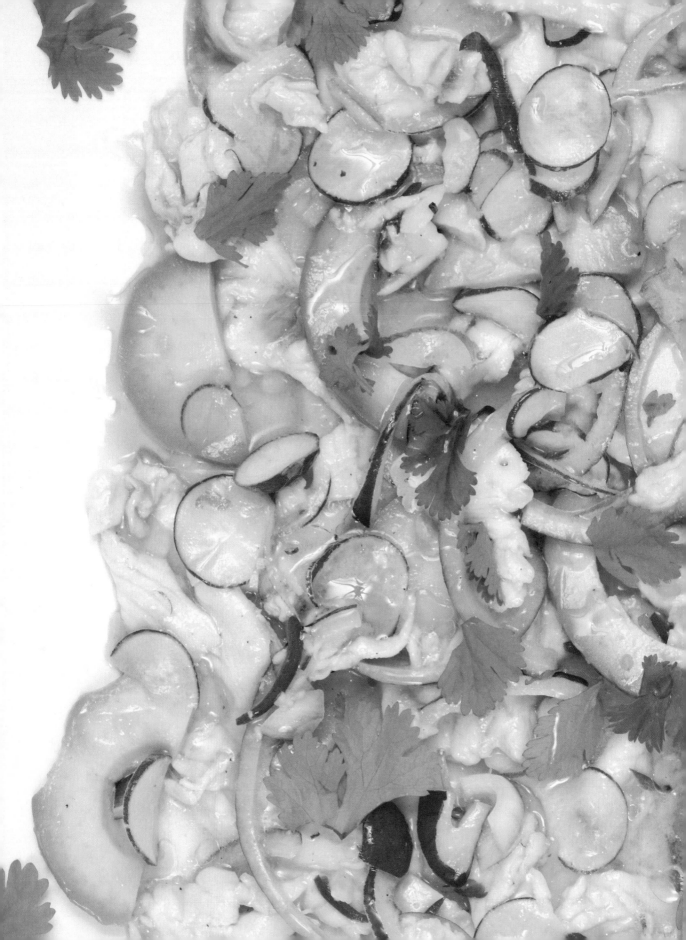

RAW FOOD

SOME OF THE GREAT SUMMER DISHES
REQUIRE NO COOKING AT ALL

Ceviche (recipe on page 148)

CEVICHE

A simple, stunning, and superfresh dish for a hot summer's day. The lemon juice "cooks" the fish delicately. Eat with a glass of white wine so cold there's a kind of mist on the side of the glass.

Feeds: 4 (as a appetizer or light lunch)
Preparation time: 15 minutes
Cooking time: 0 minutes

♥ ✓ WF GF DF

½ a **fresh red chile**
½ a **red onion**
a handful of **radishes** (the bigger each radish the better)
8 oz of **sea bass fillet** (equivalent to a 1¼ lb bass), boned and skinned
juice of 1 **lemon**
3 tablespoons **extra virgin olive oil**
1 **avocado**
a small bunch of **fresh cilantro**
sea salt & **freshly ground black pepper**

1. Seed and slice the chile into fine strips and peel and slice the red onion as fine as you can manage. Slice the radishes very thinly.

2. Finely slice the sea bass into strips and put it in a bowl with the chile, onion, and radishes, together with the lemon juice and olive oil.

3. Season well with salt and pepper—this is the most important step with ceviche. You have a very simple balance of flavors, so take time to get the seasoning just right. Add more chile, and lemon juice, if necessary.

4. Let stand for 10 minutes—and no more (less if you like it a little sushi-style). If you leave it for too long the fish will "overcook."

5. Peel the avocado and cut in half, remove the pit, and slice each half into delicate semicircles. Arrange the fish mixture on a large plate, pour over any remaining lemon marinade, and drizzle with a little extra olive oil. Sprinkle with the cilantro leaves and serve.

 TIPS

○ In Peru, this is a national dish. They often eat it as a simple lunch—*almuerzo*—with baked sweet potato. The orange color and sweet taste of the potato make a wonderful switch for the avocado in this recipe.

○ Ceviche is one of those dishes you can experiment with. Try lime juice instead of lemon. Change the fish—use scallops, raw shrimp, or salmon. Use pieces of grilled corn on the cob from the grill instead of avocado.

○ Make it your own (see page 151).

CARPACCIO WITH PARMESAN CRISP

Very quick, much easier than people think, and superimpressive (pictured on page 150).

Feeds: 4
Preparation time: 10 minutes
Cooking time: 5 minutes

✓ WF GF

½ teaspoon **coriander seeds**
½ teaspoon **cumin seeds**
½ teaspoon **sea salt**
½ teaspoon **freshly ground black pepper**
1 lb **tenderloin** or **toploin steak** (a good-quality one)
2 tablespoons **extra virgin olive oil**
a lime-size lump of **Parmesan cheese**
1 tablespoon **crème fraîche** or **fromage frais**
a handful of **arugula leaves**
1 tablespoon **balsamic vinegar**

1. Grind together the spices, salt and pepper and rub well into the steak. Sear the outside of the meat in a hot skillet for 1 minute with 1 tablespoon of the olive oil. Remove it from the skillet, let it cool, then wrap it in plastic wrap and refrigerate.

2. Grate the Parmesan superfine and sprinkle it in an even layer onto a hot nonstick saucepan. It will bubble and turn slightly golden. Slide it off with a spatula and let stand on a piece of paper towel. As it cools, it will crisp up.

3. Slice the meat finely and arrange it on a plate with spoonfuls of crème fraîche. Sprinkle the arugula on top, and drizzle with the balsamic vinegar and remaining olive oil. Season. Break the Parmesan crisp into pieces and sprinkle on top.

○ You can place the steak under plastic wrap after searing and slicing, and whack it with a rolling pin if you want it superfine. We never bother, but you can if you want to.

○ This goes wonderfully with Anchovy & Caper Miracle Sauce (recipe on page 128).

○ For variations on this theme, see page 151.

SIX WAYS WITH CEVICHE

A great ceviche requires a sharp marinated fishy element and a sweet element (the bass and avocado respectively in the main recipe on page 148). You can use the same technique to make any number of variations. These are some that we have tried in the past. Keep the onion, chile, oil, and cilantro and replace the fish, radish, and avocado with the listed ingredients.

English:
Finely sliced scallops and pea shoots.

West Indian:
Finely sliced large, raw shrimp with mango and avocado.

Peruvian:
Sea bass with small chunks of roasted sweet potato.

Scottish:
Wild salmon and very finely sliced fennel.

Vegetarian:
Zucchini, sliced thinly into tongues, using a peeler.

AND AN ADDED BONUS …

Leche de tigre (tiger's milk):
Mix the liquid that runs off the ceviche with ice-cold vodka. A great aperitif or hangover cure.

SIX WAYS WITH CARPACCIO

Once you have your basic carpaccio recipe down pat, you can play with all kinds of variations for the toppers. Our favorites include:

Classic:
Drizzled with a mustardy dressing (the one for the leek vinaigrette on page 64 works really well).

British:
Little roasted beets with horseradish cream and watercress.

Fusion:
Finely sliced chiles and a drizzle of soy sauce.

Continental:
Capers, olive oil, and baby spinach leaves.

Summer:
Finely shaved fennel in a light lemon and olive oil dressing.

Fashionable:
Parmesan shavings, olive oil, and finely sliced black truffle.

Left: Carpaccio with Parmesan Crisp

Zucchini Cannelloni

Gabriela's Raw Feast

It's always interesting to dip one's toes into the wilder shores of culinary fashion. So when our friend Gabriela—a holistic health consultant who lived for years in New York and LA—offered to cook us an entirely "raw" feast, curiosity overcame us.

The raw food movement is about much more than celery sticks. Raw evangelists eat only uncooked, unprocessed, unpasteurized, and usually organic food, which they believe is closer to our natural diet. By eliminating cooked food, they claim their bodies benefit from the vitamins, minerals, and enzymes that get destroyed in the cooking process, and, thereby, gain health and vitality.

The constraints of raw food can encourage amazing creativity: Gabriela introduced us, for instance, to delicious "dehydrated crackers" and rich creamy "casheez"—a substitute for cream cheese made from soaked and ground cashew nuts. But the dishes opposite are straightforward enough for anyone to try.

Raw Masala Carrot Dip

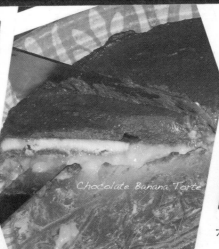

Chocolate Banana Torte

The oven has a night off

Gabriela, preparing our feast

Gabriela Garay
Holistic Health Services
gabriela@thepickyfoodie.com

thepickyfoodie.com

Vegan sushi

Raw Food Feast Menu

Gabriela's Green Smoothie
(see page 41)
......
Raw Masala Carrot Dip
(with three kinds of dehydrated crackers:
onion, rosemary, and cheesy hazelnut)
......
Vegan Mushroom Sushi
......
Zucchini Cannelloni with Casheez
in a Fresh Tomato and Herb Sauce
......
Chocolate Banana Torte

Dipping sauce for sushi rolls

RAW MASALA CARROT DIP

Makes: 4 cups
Preparation time: 10 minutes
Cooking time: 0 minutes
♥ ✓ WF DF GF V

8 **carrots** (about 1½ lb)
1 cup raw **tahini**
juice of 1 **lemon**
juice of 1 **orange**
1 teaspoon **garam masala**
3 teaspoons **ground cumin**
½ a small **onion**
a 1 inch piece of **fresh ginger**
3 **pitted dates**
⅛ cup **extra virgin olive oil**
a large handful of **fresh cilantro leaves**
sea salt and **freshly ground black pepper**

1. Wash the carrots, peel, and cut into large chunks. Put into a food processor with 1 cup of water and process until smooth.

2. Add the tahini, lemon juice, orange juice, garam masala, cumin, and a pinch of salt and process until smooth. Peel the onion and ginger, then add them and the dates, one ingredient at a time, and process again until smooth.

3. Add the oil, processing as you work, and adding up to ⅛ cup of water if you think it needs it. Season.

4. Add the cilantro leaves, reserving a few, and process once again.

5. Chop the reserved cilantro leaves and use as a garnish.

6. Serve with crackers or chunks of vegetables for dipping.

TIPS

○ If you have a high-quality blender, you can make a really smooth final texture by transferring the mixture to the blender for a final processing before serving.

○ If you can't find raw tahini, use normal tahini found in supermarkets and health stores.

RECIPE TESTED BY CRESSIDA

RAW CHOCOLATE BANANA TORTE

Start by making the bottom layer so that it has time to set in the freezer.

Feeds: 10
Preparation time: 20 minutes
Cooking time: 0 minutes
♥ ✓ WF DF GF V

⅔ cup whole **almonds**
6 **pitted dates**
⅛ cup **sunflower seeds**
a pinch of **salt**
¼ cup melted **coconut oil**
4 **bananas**
2 **avocados**
2 tablespoons **tahini**
⅛ cup **cacao powder**
½ teaspoon **vanilla powder**
2–4 teaspoons **honey**, depending on how sweet you like it

1. Combine the almonds, dates, sunflower seeds, and salt in a food processor. Melt the coconut oil in a bain-marie to avoid overheating. Once the oil has liquefied, pour it into the food processor while the engine is running. The mixture should end up as more or less one uniform ball.

2. Divide into 2 parts, one larger (about ¾), one smaller (about ¼), and put the smaller one aside. Press the larger part into an 8 inch loose-bottom cake pan with the bottom of your palm until it is about ¼ inch thick. Put it into the freezer to set while you prepare the other layers.

3. Peel the bananas, mash up 2, and cut the remaining 2 into even slices.

4. Peel the avocados and discard the pit. Place the flesh in a food processor with the tahini and blend well. Add the cacao and vanilla powder, then the honey. At the very end, dilute ever so slightly with a little water.

5. Remove the bottom layer of the torte from the freezer and cover it with the mashed bananas. At this point, roll out the second, smaller chunk of dough until it is about as thick as a pancake and gently place on top of the mashed bananas.

6. Gently arrange the sliced bananas over the entire surface.

7. Cover with the avocado layer and place in the refrigerator until you are ready to serve it.

TIPS

o For a sweeter torte, use riper bananas. If you cannot find vanilla powder, use vanilla extract.

o Watch people's faces carefully when you tell them (after they have eaten it) that it contains avocado.

SUMMER SALADS

A barbecue needs a salad as surely as Romeo needed Juliet.

These are four of our favorite simple barbecue salads, and a collection of punchy dressings.

GREEN SUNSHINE SALAD

This is a popular side dish in the restaurants—we wanted to create something simple and fresh, and the mint gives it real zing.

Feeds: 4 (as a generous side)
Preparation time: 10 minutes
Cooking time: 5 minutes
♥ ✓ WF DF GF V

2 cups **green beans**
2⅔ cups **frozen peas**
2⅔ cups **frozen edamame beans**
a large handful of **fresh mint**
½ cup **Leon House Dressing** (recipe on page 163)

1. Trim the green beans and chop them in half. Cook them briefly in boiling water, then refresh them in a bowl of cold water.

2. Defrost the peas and the edamame beans.

3. Coarsely chop the mint.

4. Drain the green beans and combine together all the ingredients.

TIPS

o You can use any mixture of green beans for this salad—frozen fava beans and Italian flat beans both work well if you can't get hold of edamame beans.

THIRTIETH BIRTHDAY PEA SALAD

Feeds: 4
Preparation time: 5 minutes
Cooking time: 10 minutes
♥ ✓ WF DF GF V

1 **red bell pepper**
1 inch piece of **fresh ginger**
2 cloves of **garlic**
6 **scallions**
2 tablespoons **extra virgin olive oil**
1 teaspoon **black mustard seeds**
1 teaspoon **red wine vinegar**
1⅔ cups **frozen peas**
a small handful of **fresh cilantro**, washed
sea salt and **freshly ground black pepper**

I first made this salad at my joint thirtieth birthday party with my friends Simon and Roly. We made it for about 150 people, dressing it by tossing it in (clean) garbage bag—a useful trick. *Henry*

1. Halve and seed the bell pepper, and cut into slices. Peel and grate the ginger and garlic. Trim the scallions and cut on the diagonal into long thin strips.

2. Heat the olive oil in a saucepan over medium heat and sauté the mustard seeds until they pop. Swirl in the garlic and ginger.

3. Add the bell pepper, stirring well until it picks up some color. Add the scallions and the vinegar. It will sizzle a bit.

4. Throw in the peas with a tiny splash of water and let defrost and warm up, stirring occasionally. You are not looking to cook them, just to get them up to room temperature.

5. Remove from the heat. Season and add the chopped cilantro.

WARM ANCHOVY, GARLIC, & POTATO SALAD

Pouring a dressing onto warm potatoes has a wonderful effect, because the potatoes soften and absorb the flavors. This dish is very addictive.

Feeds: 4
Preparation time: 5 minutes
Cooking time: 20 minutes
♥ WF GF DF

1¾ lb **new potatoes**
3 cloves of **garlic**
2 tablespoons **white wine vinegar**
1 x (2 oz) can of **anchovy fillets**
½ cup **extra virgin olive oil**
1 tablespoon finely chopped **fresh chives**
sea salt and **freshly ground black pepper**

1. Chop the potatoes in half and boil them, covered, in a large saucepan of salted water until tender.

2. Put the garlic, vinegar, and anchovies into a blender and process to form a paste. With the blender running, drizzle in the extra virgin olive oil. Season.

3. Drain the potatoes and pour the dressing over them, tossing them well.

4. Let cool for 3 minutes, then toss again. Sprinkle with the chopped chives and serve.

TIPS

○ It is a good idea to cut the potatoes in half with a fork once cooked, so that they are roughed up and absorb the anchovy dressing.

○ You can use parsley in the place of chives.

○ If you can't get hold of new potatoes, any white round or red-skinned potatoes will do. If you use bigger ones, peel them and chop them into chunks.

○ Great as a side salad at a barbecue. Make it in the morning and serve it later at room temperature.

Leon, Eastern Mediterranean, 1959

Above:
Warm Anchovy, Garlic, & Potato Salad
Below: Thirtieth Birthday Salad

Our favorite trick for creating a sumptuous green salad (other than a great salad dressing— see page 163) is to chop a lot of herbs finely and toss them in among the leaves.

QUICK GREEN SALAD

Leafy herbs all work: dill, parsley, sage, cilantro, chives, oregano, marjoram, and mint.
Add as many different types as you like to a single salad for a flavor explosion.

1

2

3

4

1 TAPENADE DRESSING

Best used to dress strong-flavored salad greens or cooked greens.

Makes ½ cup   Preparation time: 3 minutes   Cooking time: 0 minutes   ♥ ✓ WF DF GF (V if you use anchovy-free tapenade)

2 tablespoons **tapenade**
1 tablespoon **sherry vinegar**
⅓ cup **extra virgin olive oil**
sea salt and **freshly ground black pepper**

1. Put all the ingredients into a screw-top jar.
2. Screw on the lid, shake well, and check the seasoning.

2 LEON HOUSE DRESSING

Gives a real punch to old-fashioned lettuce leaves. Keeps well in the refrigerator.

Makes 2 cups   Preparation time: 3 minutes   Cooking time: 0 minutes   ♥ ✓ WF DF GF V

2 tablespoons **Dijon mustard**
⅓ cup **white wine vinegar**
1½ cups **canola oil**
sea salt and **freshly ground black pepper**

1. Blend the mustard and vinegar in a blender.
2. Keeping the blender running, slowly add the canola oil until you have a completely emulsified dressing.
3. Season carefully.

3 BALSAMIC DRESSING

Best for simple green salads with plenty of chopped herbs in them.

Makes ½ cup   Preparation time: 3 minutes   Cooking time: 0 minutes   ♥ ✓ WF DF GF V

2 tablespoons **balsamic vinegar**
  (use a nice syrupy aged one if you can)
6 tablespoons **extra virgin olive oil**
  (a good one really makes a difference)
sea salt and **freshly ground black pepper**

1. Put the ingredients straight on the salad.
2. Grind over plenty of black pepper and add a generous amount of salt.
3. Toss with vigour.

4 ASIAN DRESSING

Best on shredded vegetables—for example, shredded carrot and zucchini or finely shredded Chinese cabbage.

Makes ½ cup   Preparation time: 8 minutes   Cooking time: 0 minutes   ♥ ✓ WF DF GF V

1 fat clove of **garlic**
½ inch piece of **fresh ginger**
1 **scallion**
½ a **fresh red chile**
1 tablespoon **Thai fish sauce**
juice of ½ a **lime**
3 tablespoons **peanut oil** or
  other flavorless oil
1 tablespoon **toasted sesame oil**

1. Grate the garlic and ginger into a small, clean screw-top jar with a lid, using your finest grater.
2. Finely slice the scallion and seed and finely chop the chile. Add to the jar.
3. Measure in the fish sauce and lime juice and add the oils. Screw on the lid and shake well.

TIPS

○ You can add a little honey if you like your dressing sweet.

Three grown-up iced pops to cool you down on a hot summer's day.

Each recipe makes ice pops for 6

STRAWBERRY ICE POPS

Preparation time: 10 minutes
Freezing time: Overnight
(minimum 2½ hours)
♥ ✓ WF DF GF V

2 pints **strawberries,** hulled
3 level teaspoons **fructose**
1 tablespoon **vodka**

1. Put the strawberries, fructose, and vodka into a blender and blend until smooth.

2. Divide equally among ice pops molds and push in the sticks (or cut-off straws).

3. Put in the freezer until firm.

MANGO ICE POPS

♥ ✓ WF DF GF V

12 cups **mango flesh** (from 13 large mangoes)
3 level teaspoons **fructose**
1 tablespoon **vodka**

1. Put the mango, fructose, and vodka into a blender and blend until smooth.

2. Divide equally among ice pops molds and push in the sticks (or cut-off straws).

3. Put in the freezer until firm.

BAILEYS ICE POPS

✓ WF GF V

2 cups **heavy cream**
3 level teaspoons **fructose**
3 tablespoons **Baileys**

1. Put the cream, fructose, and Baileys into a blender and blend until smooth.

2. Divide equally among ice pops molds and push in the sticks (or cut-off straws).

3. Put in the freezer until firm.

TIPS

○ The vodka brings out the flavor of the fruit. You can omit the alcohol if you want to avoid sedating your children.

○ Create a arugula ship (see opposite)—this is difficult but rewarding. Freeze each of these ices in individual layers one after the other. Then drizzle a little melted chocolate on top (make sure the ice pop is *really* cold first), and sprinkle on some space dust or sherbet. Cool on a sheet of wax paper in the freezer.

Arugula ship ice pops. Background drawing by Madelaine Cooper.

FABULOUS

ICE POPS

HATTIE AND APPLE'S GUIDE TO COOKING WITH KIDS

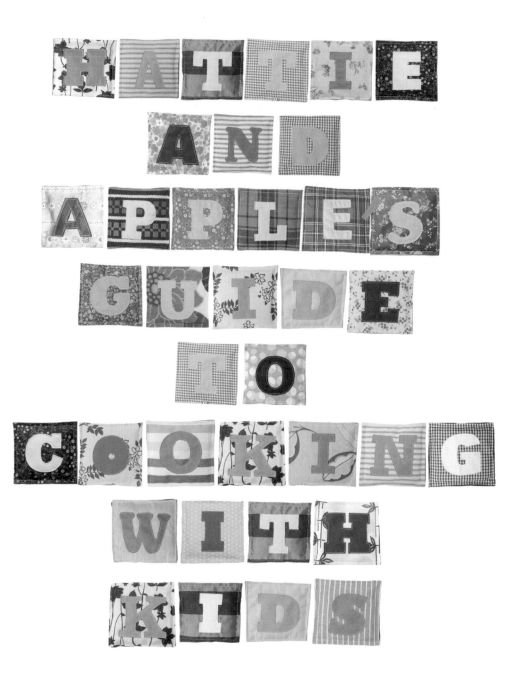

CHICKEN NUGGETS

Feeds: 4 children
Preparation time: 10 minutes
Cooking time: 15 minutes
♥ ✓ DF

2 **chicken breasts** or **boneless thighs**
1 **egg**
2 handfuls of **bread crumbs**
½ tablespoon **olive oil**

1. Preheat the oven to 350°F.

2. Cut the chicken into nugget-size pieces.

3. Crack the egg into a bowl and whisk with a fork. Put the bread crumbs on a plate. Dip the chicken pieces into the beaten egg and roll in the bread crumbs.

4. Line a baking sheet with aluminum foil or parchment paper, and arrange the chicken pieces on it. Sprinkle with the oil.

5. Place into the oven for about 15 minutes, or until the chicken coating is lightly brown and the chicken cooked through.

TIPS

o Use brown grainy bread crumbs, or a mixture of bread crumbs and crushed potato chips, for extra crunch.

OVEN FRIES

All sensible people, adults or children, like a bowl of fries every now and then, so make them the healthy way at home.

Feeds: 4 children
Preparation time: 5 minutes
Cooking time: 30 minutes
♥ WF DF GF V

500g **russet potatoes**
3 tablespoons **olive oil** or **vegetable oil**
sea salt and **freshly ground black pepper**

1. Preheat the oven to 350°F.

2. Wash the potatoes under cold running water and remove any gnarly parts. Leaving the skins on, cut the potatoes into thin batons.

3. Put the batons into an ovenproof dish, cover with the oil, season, and and toss well.

4. Place the dish in the oven and cook for 30 minutes, or until the fries are crisp.

5. Do not serve the fries until they have cooled down enough for small mouths!

TIPS

o Serve with homemade chicken nuggets, fish sticks, or dip into hummus.

o Try different seasonings, such as chopped thyme, ground allspice, or garam masala.

Oven fries in the bowl, fish sticks and chicken nuggets on the plate

FRESH FISH STICKS

Forget buying fish sticks: even the supermarket ones you can get nowadays won't taste as good as if you make them yourself. Make a double batch and freeze the rest.

Makes: 25 mini fish sticks
Preparation time: 15 minutes
Cooking time: 10 minutes

♥ ✓

10 oz **fish** (I use salmon fillet)
1 extra-large **egg**
¼ cup **flour**
1 cup dried **bread crumbs**
grated **Parmesan cheese**—optional
sea salt and **freshly ground pepper**—optional
2 tablespoons **olive oil** or **canola oil**

1. Check your fish carefully for bones.

2. With a sharp knife cut the fish into stick shapes, about ½ inch wide and 1½ inches long.

3. Crack the egg into a clean bowl, and whisk lightly. Put the flour into another bowl, and the bread crumbs into a third bowl. Add Parmesan and seasoning to the flour if you desire.

4. Working in batches, coat the fish first in the flour, then dip in the egg, and finally roll in the bread crumbs.

5. Heat the oil in a nonstick skillet and gently sauté the fish sticks until golden.

6. Serve when cool enough to eat.

 TIPS

○ You can use any fish you like—I like salmon. And if you prefer not to use white flour, feel free to use any kind.

ARTHUR'S FAVORITE DUCK & LETTUCE WRAPS

A healthy and fun dish for the children to help make.

Feeds: 4 children
Preparation time: 5 minutes
Cooking time: 25 minutes

WF DF GF

1 **cucumber**
2 **Boston lettuce**
1 **duck breast**
olive oil
a jar of **plum sauce**
sea salt and **freshly ground pepper**

1. Preheat the oven to 375°F. Cut the cucumber into batons and put into a bowl. Separate the lettuce leaves and put into a second bowl.

2. Season the duck breast, and add a dash of olive oil, and roast for about 25 minutes, until the skin is crispy. Separate the cooked meat into little pieces, using 2 forks.

3. Get the children to make packages, wrapping the duck and cucumber in the lettuce leaves, and serve the plum sauce on the side in a small bowl.

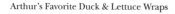

GEORGE PICKARD'S CHEESE & HAM MUFFINS

A great snack for when you get back from school instead of sugary cookies.

Makes: 12
Preparation time: 15 minutes
Cooking time: 20 minutes

6 slices of **ham**
1⅔ cups **cheddar cheese**
5 tablespoons **butter**
1 **egg**
1 cup **milk**
2⅛ cups **all-purpose flour**
3½ teaspoons **baking powder**
½ teaspoon **paprika**
a pinch of **sea salt**

1. Preheat the oven to 375°F. Lightly grease a muffin pan.

2. Cut the ham into ½ inch chunks, and shred the cheddar or chop it coarsely. Cut the butter into pieces. Beat the egg in a bowl with the milk.

3. Sift the flour, baking powder, paprika, and salt into a large mixing bowl, and rub the butter into the flour until it looks like bread crumbs.

4. Add the ham and cheese, then pour in the egg and milk mixture and mix thoroughly.

5. Spoon into the muffin pan and cook in the oven for 20 minutes.

6. Place on a wire rack to cool.

George loves cooking and learned this recipe at school—I often find him in the kitchen making these on his own. Sadly, they don't last very long, because they are delicious!
Apple

FRIENDS & FAMILY RECIPES

George, High House Farm, 2004

LAMB & APRICOT BALLS

A quick and easy dinner. Delicious with mashed sweet potatoes.

Makes: about 25 meatballs
Preparation time: 15 minutes
Cooking time: 10–15 minutes
✓ WF DF GF

1 **onion**
⅓ cup **dried apricots**
3 tablespoons **olive oil**
1 lb **ground lamb**
1 medium **egg**
sea salt and **freshly ground black pepper**—optional

1. Peel the onion and put into a food processor with the apricots. Process until they are both finely chopped. If you don't have a food processor, chop them very finely by hand.

2. Heat 1 tablespoon of the olive oil in a small skillet. Add the onions and apricots and cook gently for 10–15 minutes, stirring occasionally to make sure they don't burn.

3. Put the ground lamb into a large bowl, add the egg, and mix with your hands. Add the onions and apricots to the lamb, and mix again. If you want to add salt and pepper, do this now.

4. With clean, wet hands, roll the lamb mixture into small balls, and set them aside on a plate.

5. Heat the rest of the olive oil in a skillet, and gently fry the lamb balls until golden and cooked through. This should take about 10 minutes. Let them cool down a little before serving to children.

TIPS

○ You can add herbs and very finely chopped spinach to the lamb mixture if you want to sneak in some veg.

○ Depending on the children, and how exotic their palate is, add ground cumin and cinnamon for an extra twist.

○ If you do not want to sauté these, you can bake them in the oven at 350°F for about 15 minutes.

○ Perfect for the freezer and can even be cooked from frozen.

Ned reading the papers, summer 2009

FRIENDS & FAMILY RECIPES

I started to make meatballs for my son Ned when he was about eight months old to get him interested in feeding himself. It didn't really work, because he still likes his minions to spoon-feed him while he reclines in his chair, but he does occasionally feed himself crispy fried or oven-baked foods such as these. *Hattie*

TEATIME &

Illustration by
Flora McEvedy

ELEVENSES

Tea and elevenses:
two great British institutions.
Yet on busy days, you might not even notice yourself
indulging in one or another. Too easily, snacking becomes
something you do unthinkingly to stop yourself from
falling asleep at your desk.

Done right, however, a snack is more than just a small energy
boost. It can be a real treat, a shared ritual with friends,
a moment of escapism.

MOM'S CHOCOLATE & FRUIT COOKIE CAKE

An old-fashioned no-cook way to make a rich and crunchy cake; it can be stored in the refrigerator in a plastic container for weeks if in the unlikely event that you don't eat it all straight away.

Feeds: 10–12
Preparation time: 10 minutes
Cooking time: 10 minutes

Jossy

1½ sticks **butter**
3 tablespoons **honey**
8 oz **semisweet chocolate**
25 **gingersnaps** (about 6 oz)
25 **butter cookies** (about 6 oz)
⅔ cup soft **dried apricots**
4 **dried figs**
½ cup large **seedless raisins**
zest and juice of 1 **orange**
a dusting of **confectioners' sugar**

1. Butter a deep 8–9 inch diameter cake pan (or any shaped pan will do) but not one with a loose bottom.

2. Put the butter, honey, and broken-up chocolate into a fairly large saucepan over low heat and stir until smoothly melted together.

3. Coarsely crush the gingersnaps and butter cookies roughly, either briefly in a food processor or with a rolling pin.

4. Chop the apricots and figs into small pieces and stir into the melted chocolate mixture, along with the raisins, crushed cookies, and orange zest and juice. Mix together thoroughly, then turn into the prepared cake pan and spread level.

5. Chill in the refrigerator until set, then dip the pan briefly in very hot water and turn out onto a serving plate. Let stand at room temperature for at least 30 minutes before eating, then sprinkle the top with confectioners' sugar with a sifter or through a fine strainer and cut into thin slices with a sharp knife.

TIPS

o Don't worry too much about the type of cookies and fruit. Feel free to mix and match, depending on what is available.

o Wonderful with a touch of candied or ground ginger.

From the top: Jossy's Casablanca Cakes;
Great Granny's Rock Buns;
Hannah's Welsh Cakes;
Mom's Chocolate & Fruit Cookie Cake

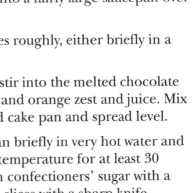

The Dimbleby family in the Dordogne, 1976

Mom used to make this when we were kids. It is nostalgic and very nice. When we were taking the photographs for the book, we left a whole cake on the side and in an hour noticed that it had gone. No one ever confessed.
Henry

FRIENDS & FAMILY RECIPES

JOSSY'S CASABLANCA CAKES

Perfect with ice cream (pictured on page 178).

Makes: 25–30
Preparation time: 15 minutes
Cooking time: 12 minutes

DF

⅛ cup **almonds**, with skins
1 **lemon**
1 **extra-large egg**
¾ cup **confectioners' sugar**
½ teaspoon **baking powder**
½ cup **semolina**
extra **confectioners' sugar**
  for dipping

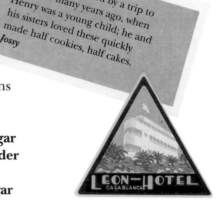

These were inspired by a trip to Morocco many years ago, when Henry was a young child; he and his sisters loved these quickly made half cookies, half cakes.
Jossy

RECIPE TESTED BY JO & JAMES

1. Preheat the oven to 325°F.

2. Put the almonds into a food processor and grind as finely as possible. Finely grate the lemon rind.

3. Beat the egg with the confectioners' sugar until very pale. Stir in the baking powder, semolina, ground almonds, and lemon rind. Mix thoroughly.

4. Butter a large baking sheet and put some sifted confectioners' sugar into a small bowl. Dampen your hands, take a piece of the mixture, and form a ball the size of a large marble. Dip one side of the ball into the confectioners' sugar and place it on the baking sheet, sugar side up.

5. Continue like this with the rest of the mixture, spacing the balls 2 inches apart because they spread a lot—you will probably have to cook them in two batches.

6. Bake the cakes in the center of the oven for 10–12 minutes, until only very pale brown. Ease carefully off the baking sheet with a spatula and cool on a rack.

HANNAH'S WELSH CAKES

Hannah and Xander put their faith (and some money) into Leon before we opened our first restaurant. They are both incurable enthusiasts and excellent cooks.

Makes: 12
Preparation time: 20 minutes
Cooking time: 10 minutes

V

1¾ cups **all-purpose flour**
2¾ teaspoons **baking powder**
1 stick **butter**
⅛ cup **sugar**
⅛ cup **golden raisins** or **dried currants**
1 **egg**

Hannah & her mom, 1978

My mom's recipe from the Teifi Valley. When we visited Mount Vernon, George Washington's home in Virginia, there was a familiar smell of baking—it came from a group of actors who were cooking over an open fire, and I recognized their baked goods as being similar to the Welsh cakes I had eaten as a child.
Hannah

FRIENDS & FAMILY RECIPES

1. Sift the flour into a bowl, then rub in the butter until it is like fine bread crumbs.

2. Add the sugar and dried fruit, and mix well. Beat the egg, add to the bowl, and mix well until the dough makes a ball.

3. Knead for a few minutes, then roll out on a floured board until ½ inch thick. Cut into circular shapes.

4. Heat a little vegetable oil in a skillet and cook the cakes on both sides for about 6–8 minutes in total. Be careful not to let them burn.

5. Let cool (see picture on page 178).

GREAT GRANNY'S ROCK CAKES

Makes: 12
Preparation time: 10 minutes
Cooking time: 15 minutes
v

1½ cups **all-purpose flour**
6 tablespoons **butter**
⅔ cup **granulated sugar**
a pinch of **ground cinnamon**
1 teaspoon **baking powder**
½ cup **golden raisins** or **dried currants**
1 medium **egg**

Janet stepping out in Seaford, 1959

1. Preheat the oven to 350°F.

2. Sift the flour into a large, clean bowl. Cut the butter into chunks and rub it in until it looks like bread crumbs.

3. Add the sugar, cinnamon, baking powder, and golden raisins and mix thoroughly.

4. Whisk the egg and add it to the bowl, mixing it in with your hands. The mixture will seem dry but don't be alarmed—this is how rock buns are supposed to be.

5. Lightly flour a baking sheet and arrange the mixture in 12 mounds, leaving plenty of space between for them to spread.

6. Bake for 15 minutes, or until golden brown (see picture on page 178).

The Lewis family in Beach Cottages, 1960

Our granny and her sister Betty used to make these from a recipe inherited from their grandmother, which makes us fifth-generation rock-bun makers. They should be firm when cool.
Hattie

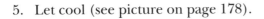

SALLY DOLTON'S GRANOLA BARS

Sally is a Leon regular who sent us this recipe for her granola bars when we mentioned that we were writing a second cookbook. They are really, really good.

Makes: 16
Preparation time: 15 minutes
Cooking time: 20 minutes
♥ ✓ DF V

1½ cups **dried fruit** (e.g. apricots, figs, dates, pears etc.—a mixture or choose just one)
½ cup **nuts** (e.g. cashew nuts)
½ cup **seeds** (e.g. pumpkin seeds, sunflower seeds)
1 teaspoon **ground cinnamon**
⅓ cup **fruit juice** (e.g. apple or grape)
2 tablespoons **honey**
½ cup **whole-wheat flour**
1⅓ cups rolled **oats**

1. Preheat the oven to 375°F.

2. Put the dried fruit into a food processor and process until well chopped. Do the same with the nuts. Put the fruit, nuts, seeds, and cinnamon into a bowl.

3. Heat together the fruit juice and honey in a saucepan large enough to eventually contain all the ingredients, until the honey is dissolved. Add the flour and oats, and stir in the fruit and nuts.

4. Smooth the dough into a 10 x 12 inch baking pan about 1 each deep. If the pan is not nonstick, it is wise to line it with parchment paper.

5. Bake in the oven for 20 minutes—longer if you would like your bars more crunchy.

6. Let cool, then cut into rectangular bars. They will keep for 2 weeks in an airtight container.

 TIPS

○ Try adding a handful of grated fresh ginger.

FRIENDS & FAMILY RECIPES

Nigel, Timmy, and Sally gorging strawberry in 1979

Glasgow Banana Bread (left) and Sally Dolton's Granola Bars

GLASGOW BANANA BREAD

A wholesome fruity loaf (pictured on page 183).

Feeds: 4–6
Preparation time: 15 minutes
Cooking time: 30 minutes

v

2 **medium eggs** (or 1 large)
1 stick **unsalted butter**, melted
2–3 tablespoons **whole milk**, or more if needed
4 very ripe **bananas**
2½ cups **spelt flour**
1 teaspoon **baking soda**
2 tablespoons **wheat germ**—optional
¼ cup **molasses** or ⅛ cup **firmly packed dark brown sugar**
1 cup **cashew nuts**
⅔ cup **poppy seeds**
zest of 1 **lemon**
a pinch of **salt**

1. Heat the oven to 350°F, and grease and line a 9 x 5 x 3 inch loaf pan.

2. Beat together the eggs, melted butter, and milk. Coarsely mash up the bananas and add to the mixture.

3. In a separate bowl, sift together the spelt flour and baking soda. Stir in the wheat germ (if using), sugar, cashew nuts, poppy seeds, lemon zest, and salt.

4. Gently fold the egg mixture into the dry ingredients—do not overstir.

5. The batter should be a good dropping consistency—firm enough to stick to a spoon, but able to drop off if you turn it upside down. Add a little more flour or milk to get the correct consistency.

6. Put into the greased pan and bake for about 30 minutes, or until a fork inserted into the center comes out cleanly.

TIPS

o If you would like the bread to have a Polish feel, add more poppy seeds.

o You can also add dates, prunes or raisins, or some shredded carrot, to diversify the banana flavor.

o Serve it in slices, spread with butter.

Leon's opening day, July 2004, by Liza Dimbleby

My elder sister is an artist who lives in Glasgow but she heads to Leon whenever she is down south. On the day we opened in Carnaby Street in London, she sat in the front of the restaurant sketching us for posterity.
Henry   LEON 2004

HENRY'S QUICK CHOCOLATE CAKE

This was the first cake I ever made, when I was about fifteen.

Feeds: 8
Preparation time: 10 minutes
Cooking time: 30 minutes
✓ WF GF V

8 **large eggs**
14 oz **dark chocolate** (70 percent cocoa solids)
1½ sticks **butter**
2 tablespoons **superfine** or **granulated sugar**
1½ cups **crème fraîche**
zest of 1 **lemon**
pinch of **sea salt**

1. Preheat your oven to 350°F, and butter two 7 inch circular cake pans. Separate the eggs, putting the yolks into a clean bowl and the whites into another. Whisk the egg yolks with a pinch of salt.

2. Melt the chocolate and butter in a large, heatproof bowl placed over a saucepan of gently simmering water. Do not let the chocolate get too hot. Let cool for a couple of minutes, then fold the egg yolks into the chocolate and butter mixture.

3. Whisk the egg whites to stiff peaks, then whisk in the sugar. Fold them gently into the chocolate and egg yolk mixture. Pour the batter into the cake pans, and cook in the oven for 15 minutes. Let the cakes cool on a rack (or in the refrigerator).

4. In a clean bowl, mix together the crème fraîche and lemon zest, and use this to sandwich together the cakes.

5. To decorate the cake, cut a shape out of cardstock, put it on top of the cake, and dust the top with confectioners' sugar. Remove the card, leaving a nice shape in silhouette.

TIPS

○ This cake is definitely grown-up—it's too strong for most young taste buds. You can add up to three times the quantity of sugar if you have a sweeter tooth.

My mom used to make a cake similar to this and it has been adapted over the years. It is a supersimple, dark, rich, and low-sugar cake.
Henry

The first unveiling of the Leon Salted Caramel Banana Split (really)

DESSERTS

DESSERT IS THE MOMENT
IN THE FEAST THAT
MAKES EVERYONE GO:
"WOW!"

CARAMELIZED PEAR FLAMBÉ *with quick real custard*

The custard method in this dish is another great tip from our friend Claire "Cakes." By using more cream and, critically, heating the sugar with the cream instead of adding it to the egg yolks, you eliminate the nervous stage of heating the custard over the stove and waiting for it to thicken, or, more often than not in my case, scramble. I never used to make custard, but I make it all the time now. *Henry*

Feeds: 4
Preparation time: 10 minutes
Cooking time: 20 minutes

WF GF V

For the custard
5 **egg yolks**
1 **vanilla bean**
2 cups **heavy cream**
½ cup **milk**
1 cup **granulated sugar**
sea salt

For the pears
1 large tablespoon **unsalted butter**
4 **pears**
2 tablespoons **packed brown sugar**
3 tablespoons **brandy** or **Cognac**, heated to boiling point

1. The eggs need to be at room temperature for this recipe.

2. Halve the vanilla bean lengthwise and put it in a saucepan with the cream, milk, and granulated sugar. Bring to a boil, stirring to make sure the sugar dissolves. Take the pan off the heat, and let it sit for 5 minutes.

3. Meanwhile, put the egg yolks into a blender and blend for 2 minutes, or until they turn creamy. Add a small pinch of salt.

4. Bring the cream back to a boil and pour it slowly onto the eggs, blending as you work. Assuming that the cream is good and hot and the eggs not too cold, the result should be great not-too-thick custard. (If you want to make it thicker, you can pour it into a pan and heat it gently on the stove, but you shouldn't need to.)

5. Peel, core, and halve the pears. Put a wide skillet over high heat. Add the butter, then the pears, and toss until well coated. Sprinkle with the brown sugar. Toss for another 4 minutes, until tinged with brown, well coated with the caramel, and tender.

6. Get everyone's attention, stand back, and pour in the brandy or Cognac—it should flame. When the flames have gone out, serve with the custard.

FRIENDS & FAMILY
RECIPES

LEON SALTED CARAMEL BANANA SPLIT

Feeds: 6
Preparation time: 10 minutes
Cooking time: 10 minutes
WF GF V

1 cup organic **slivered almonds**
2 tablespoons organic **confectioners' sugar**
6 Fairtrade **bananas**
2 cups organic **heavy cream**
½ cup **granulated sugar**
2 cups organic **vanilla ice cream**
1 cup organic **strawberry ice cream**
1 oz organic **dark chocolate**
sea salt

1. Heat the almonds in a nonstick skillet with the confectioners' sugar until they turn golden and the sugar has caramelized. Put into a bowl and set aside.

2. Halve the bananas lengthwise and lay two halves on each plate.

3. Beat 1½ cups of the cream until thick. Put into a pastry bag (a squirty cream thing available online, saves time here).

4. Heat the granulated sugar in a saucepan until it has melted and caramelized, but is not too dark. Add the remaining ½ cup of cream and stir well. It will froth right up. Heat through to make sure all the sugar has melted into the cream, stirring occasionally. Add a good pinch of salt.

5. Put 2 scoops of vanilla and one of strawberry ice cream onto each split banana.

6. Drizzle the ice cream with the caramel. Pipe the cream on top, sprinkle with the almonds, grate some chocolate over it and serve.

 TIPS

o For the truly classic split, top each scoop of ice cream with a candied cherry.

o In the restaurants, we use a black currant compote alongside the caramel as a second sauce.

RECIPE TESTED BY. TOM

LONDON W1F 7JE
LEON.
35-36 Gt. MARLBOROUGH St.
Fair Trade & Organic
NOME DEL. PASSEGGERO
BAGAGLIAIO

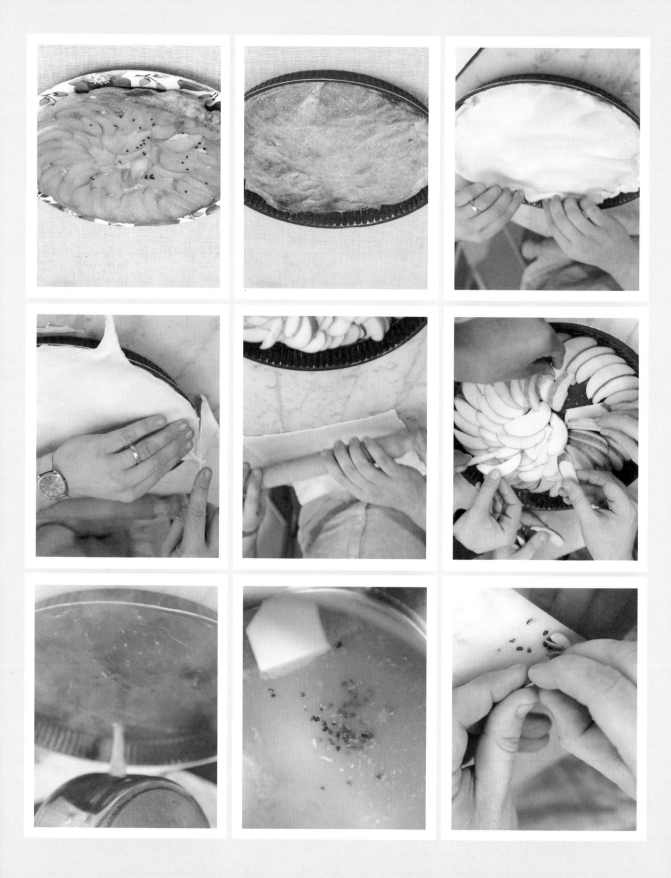

UPSIDE-DOWN APPLE & CARDAMOM TART

The flavor of the cardamom transforms this simple apple tart.

Feeds: 4
Preparation time: 10 minutes
Cooking time: 30 minutes
v

3 **cardamom pods**
juice of 1 **orange**
¼ cup **firmly packed brown sugar**
40g **butter**
4 **cooking apples** (about 1½ lb)
1 ready-to-bake sheet of **puff pastry**

1. Preheat the oven to 350°F.

2. Crush the cardamom pods and keep the little seeds. In a saucepan, heat the orange juice, sugar, butter, and cardamom seeds until thick and bubbly. Pour the syrup into a 10 inch tart pan (obviously it cannot be one with a push-out bottom or it will seep though and go everywhere).

3. Quarter the apples and cut out the cores. Cut each quarter into thin slices and arrange symmetrically on top of the syrup in the tart pan.

4. Roll out your pastry and lay it over the top of the apples in the pan. Cut off the excess around the edges. Sprinkle a little more sugar on top, if you desire.

5. Place the pan in the oven for 30 minutes, or until the pastry has risen and is golden. Put a serving plate on top, hold it tightly and flip the whole thing over. Tap the bottom of the pan to make sure that all the apple slices are on the plate, and remove it. A magically neat and tidy tart will appear.

TIPS

o Serve with cream or Quick Real Custard (see page 190).

o This is one of those versatile recipes. You can use almost any fruit—pears, plums, apricots, nectarines, peaches, and oranges all work well. You can also play with the syrup: try a red wine syrup with star anise and plums. White wine, vanilla, and nectarine make a subtle combination; with oranges, try using prepared rolled dough pie crust and a really sticky syrup made with a little molasses as well as sugar.

o When using soft fruit in this tart, it is better if the fruit is slightly underripe.

RECIPE TESTED BY: BAMBI

RECIPE TESTED BY: PETRA

RECIPE TESTED BY: KATE

SPICED RED WINE SYRUP

A little bit of class. Boil up 2 cups red wine with ½ cup fructose, 1 cinnamon stick, 4 cardamom pods, and 2 star anise. Reduce to a syrup.

MARS BAR SAUCE

The devil may claim y
Simply melt 3 Mars b
tell a soul. Stir thorou
well. It should take a

stick
n oiled
whole
ash

ised
it

DRESSING UP *store-bought ice cream*

One of the simplest ways to create a sensational dessert is to buy vanilla ice cream and dress it up. Here are some of our usual suspects:

HAZELNUT CRACKNELL

Sweet and crunchy. Melt 1 cup sugar in a non[stick] pan. Toss in ½ cup hazelnuts and pour onto a[ ] sheet of wax paper. When it is cold, wrap the [whole] thing in a dish towel and give it a satisfying sm[ash] with a rolling pin.

CARAMELIZED BISCUITS

Sweet and crispy. Crush 5 cookies and heat in a nonstick saucepan with 2 tablespoons sugar until the sugar has melted. Stir often and watch it carefully to make sure it doesn't burn.

POLICE LINE DO NOT CROSS NOTHING TO SEE HERE KEEP MOVING POLICE LINE

DO NOT CROSS NOTHING TO SEE HERE KEEP MOVING POLICE LINE DO NOT CROSS

syrup. Toss in 2½ cups mixed berries and
juices are starting to thicken. (You can add
nom—for extra flavor if you desire.)

4'6"
4'0"
3'6"
3'0"
2'6"
2'0"
1'6"
1'0"

Quick
Berry Compote

If you want to
make your own
homemade ice
cream, see the
recipes on
pages 273–74.

..u, but this is heaven on earth.
..s in ⅔ cup heavy cream and don't
..hly to make sure they have blended
..ut 10 minutes.

QUICK BERRY COMPOTE

Heat ¼ cup water and ¼ cup sugar in a saucepan until they make
cook for a couple of minutes, until the fruit has softened and th..
some sweet spice—such as vanilla, star anise, cinnamon, or carda..

RUM & RAISIN

One for the grown-ups.
Heat 1 cup rum with
2 tablespoons of raisins
or golden raisins and
2 tablespoons caster
sugar. Set the alcohol
alight and let the flame
burn for a few minutes.
Reduce to a syrupy
consistency, which
should take about
15 minutes.

PIERRE'S PAIN PERDU

Literally "lost bread," this is a great French way to use up stale bread, and is even better made with brioche.

Feeds: 4
Preparation time: 5 minutes
Cooking time: 12 minutes

1 (stale) **baguette**
⅔ cup **milk**
2 tablespoons **butter**, plus a little extra
3–4 tablespoons **firmly packed light brown sugar**

1. Cut the bread into 1¼-inch-thick diagonal slices. Put the slices into a dish where they will all fit tightly, then pour over the milk and let stand for 10 minutes so that they absorb all the milk.

2. Gently heat the butter in a large skillet. When it starts to foam, sprinkle each piece of bread on one side with half the sugar and put the slices into the skillet, sugar side down to caramelize.

3. After about 3–4 minutes, sprinkle with the remaining sugar, then turn over the slices to caramelize the other side.

4. The pain perdu should become nicely caramelized. When it's ready, add another small pat of butter to the skillet just before serving.

TIPS

- Add chopped dried fruit, such as apricots and golden raisins, to the bread when you sprinkle with the sugar.
- You can also flambé this dessert with Calvados, applejack, or brandy.
- Great with crème fraîche and fruit compote, or vanilla ice cream.

My friend Pierre loves desserts. At a dinner I cooked for him the other day, he was so disappointed that there wasn't any dessert that he got up and cooked this himself. It was mighty fine. *Henry*

FRIENDS & FAMILY RECIPES

Pierre

Amaretti & Raspberry
Dessert is a real
skier's special—
always a regular dish
when I was a girl in
Val d'Isère. The
wonderful John
Yates Smith always
thought this was
great! So easy yet
very impressive!
Apple

FRIENDS & FAMILY
RECIPES

MIXED FRUIT *with Greek yogurt & brown sugar*

A straightforward dessert that can be made a few hours in advance. People always assume that it involves some complicated brûlée action, which is pleasing.

Feeds: 4
Preparation time: 10 minutes
Cooking time: 0 minutes
WF GF V

1 large ripe **mango**
1 **kiwi**
⅔ cup **blueberries** or **blackberries**
⅔ cup hulled sliced **strawberries**
1 **passion fruit**
2 cups **Greek yogurt**
3–4 tablespoons **firmly packed dark brown sugar**

1. Peel and chop the mango and kiwi into cubes and place in a large mixing bowl.

2. Add the berries and the passion fruit seeds and mix well.

3. Choose an attractive serving bowl, or individual bowls if you want, and spoon in the chopped fruit.

4. Top generously with the Greek yogurt, so that it covers all the fruit in a thick layer.

5. Sprinkle with the brown sugar—it will start to soak into the yogurt, but you will notice that some remains in clumps and forms delicious toffeelike blobs.

TIPS

o Add more sugar if you like it swimming in the dessert.

o If you are making this in advance, you can either add the sugar just before serving, or add it earlier, let it soak into the yogurt, and add extra at the last minute.

o Use any combination of fruit. Berries and pitted fruits work the best.

APPLE'S BREATHTAKINGLY QUICK CHOCOLATE CUPS

Makes: 6 little cups
Preparation time: 5 minutes, plus 2 hours in the refrigerator
Cooking time: 0 hours
WF GF V

1 cup **heavy cream**
⅛ cup **caster sugar**
8 oz **dark chocolate**
1 teaspoon **vanilla extract**
2 **egg yolks**

1. Heat the cream and sugar in a saucepan and bring to a boil. Stir well to dissolve the sugar.

2. Chop the chocolate into small chunks and put into a food processor with the vanilla extract and egg yolks.

3. When the cream is simmering, start the processor and pour it in. When smooth, pour the mixture into small coffee cups or ramekins and refrigerate for at least 2 hours.

APPLE'S AMARETTI & RASPBERRY DESSERT

This takes no time at all and, like Apple, looks spectacular.

Feeds: 4
Preparation time: 10 minutes
Cooking time: 0 minutes v

1¼ cups **heavy cream**
1¼ cups **crème fraîche** or **Greek yogurt**
1 teaspoon **vanilla extract**
20 **amaretti cookies**
1⅔ cups **raspberries**

1. Beat the cream until thick but still pourable, like a custard.

2. Add the crème fraîche and vanilla extract and mix gently.

3. Crush the amaretti cookies and set aside a few for the top of the dish. Layer most of the raspberries with the amaretti and cream in glasses or a glass dish, then repeat the layers.

4. Finish with the rest of the raspberries and sprinkle with the reserved amaretti.

TIPS

o Make this the night before, or at least 4 hours before your guests arrive.

CLAIRE'S RHUBARB & AMARETTI TART

This tart looks crazy when you put it into the oven with its beehive of rhubarb stacked on top—but it comes out a simple and impressive finale to a good Sunday dinner.

Feeds: 6
Preparation time: 5 minutes
Cooking time: 30–35 minutes
*

1 ready-to-bake sheet of **puff pastry**, fresh or frozen
17 **amaretti** cookies
1 lb **rhubarb**
½ cup **sugar**

1. Heat the oven to 400°F.

2. Unroll the pastry and place it on a well-greased baking sheet that has been lined with parchment paper. Fold over the sides to make an edge and press down with a fork. Crumble the amaretti cookies and sprinkle over the bottom of the tart.

3. Cut the rhubarb stems in half, then slice into long thin strips and put into a bowl.

4. When you are ready to cook the tart, toss the rhubarb in the sugar and immediately stack it on top of the pastry and put it into the oven. If you wait, it will start to produce a lot of liquid.

5. Cook for 35–40 minutes, until the pastry is a light golden color.

 TIPS

o If you are using frozen pastry, allow time for it to defrost. If it's not already rolled, roll it out into a rectangle about 14 x 10 inches.

o Serve with cream or Quick Real Custard (see page 190).

o Brush the pastry with beaten egg yolk before cooking for a glazed finish.

- Life is too short for most people to make puff pastry, and the store-bought versions are excellent. Look out for one that uses pure butter.

- The ends of some of the rhubarb strips may turn a little black. You can snip these off with scissors if you want it to look perfect.

- About halfway through the baking time, I usually press the fruit down a little with the back of a spoon. At this point, it has softened and has started to release juices. Pressing the fruit down will keep the rhubarb from drying out.

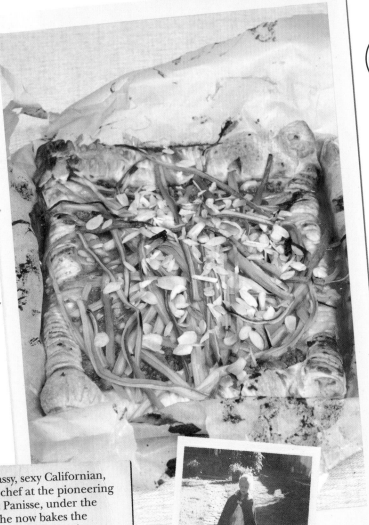

Claire is a great baker. A sassy, sexy Californian, she used to work as pastry chef at the pioneering American restaurant Chez Panisse, under the tutelage of Alice Waters. She now bakes the best cupcakes in London, and sells them in the East End's Broadway market. She made us this tart one Sunday lunchtime. It took her about 3 minutes and was sensational.
Henry

RECIPE TESTED BY · LILLIE & PETRA ·

201

Claire in her favorite red cape, age of 5

Illustration by
Flora McEvedy

FOOD

People get too worked up about throwing parties. All you need is lovely people, decent food, music, and booze. And if any of the former isn't up to scratch, judicious application of the latter will hide the cracks. These easy snacks should make your party go with a …

BANG!

70s Party

A party spread made up from the guilty secrets of friends and family.

Laura with her siblings and grandparents, 1986

Laura's smokin' mackerel dip with melba toast

♥ ✓

Serve with melba toast, platform shoes, and flares.

Laura and her sister "Party Polly" have been helping us organize parties and events for Leon since we opened.

FEEDS: 8
PREPARATION TIME: 10 MINUTES
COOKING TIME: 0 MINUTES

4 fillets **smoked mackerel**—about 12 oz
1 **fresh red chile**
zest and juice of ½ a **lime**
pinch of **ground cumin**
2 tablespoons **horseradish cream**
1 cup **cream cheese**
10 slices of **sliced white bread**
sea salt and **freshly ground black pepper**

1. Skin the mackerel, break it up into small pieces and put it into a bowl.
2. Seed the chile, chop it finely, and add it to the mackerel.
3. Add the lime zest and juice, cumin, horseradish, and cream cheese.
4. Toast the bread in a toaster and cut off the crusts. Split the bread horizontally through the middle and toast the untoasted side of each slice under the broiler.
5. Serve with the mackerel dip and crunchy carrot sticks.

RECIPE TESTED BY GEORGIE

Everything can be made in advance except for the puff pastry swirls, which are best eaten straight from the oven.

Xander's puff pastry swirls

Party savories recipe
2

FEEDS: 8
PREPARATION TIME: 20 MINUTES
COOKING TIME: 25 MINUTES

Xander has been a long-standing Leon lover. He is also a great host. If you are lucky enough to be invited to his for dinner, you will probably get these as a canapé.

1 cup pitted **ripe black olives**
⅛ cup **capers**
½ (2 oz) can **anchovies**
2 ready-to-bake sheets of frozen **puff pastry**
2 large pinches of **dried red pepper flakes**
10 **sun-dried tomatoes**
1 **egg,** beaten
freshly ground black pepper

1. Preheat the oven to 425°F.
2. Drain the olives, capers, and anchovies and coarsely chop them together.
3. Roll out each sheet of puff pastry to a thickness of ¼ inch in a long rectangle. With the long side of the rectangle facing you, spread half the olive mixture evenly onto each pastry, leaving a 1¼ inch border around the edge. Season with pepper.
4. Sprinkle the red pepper flakes over the mixture. Slice the sun-dried tomatoes and sprinkle with those, too. Gently roll up each pastry into a log. Seal the edge by dampening it with water. Refrigerate for 30 minutes.
5. Using a sharp knife and a sawing motion, cut off disks ½ inch thick and place them on a well greased baking sheet, leaving plenty of room between each one for them to spread.
6. Brush the disks with beaten egg and bake for 20 minutes. They may need another 5 minutes to brown the centers.

RECIPE TESTED BY PETRA

TIPS You can make the logs in advance and freeze them until required and then just slice and cook from frozen.

Xander and his family, Ireland, 1979

A chef I met a long time ago gave me this recipe. I did it for a drinking party and people got VERY intoxicated but loved them.
Jossy

Jossy's Vodka, chili cherry tomatoes

4 cups **cherry tomatoes**
⅔ cup **sherry**
1½ cup **vodka**
1 teaspoon **cayenne pepper**
sea salt and **freshly ground black pepper**

1. Wash the cherry tomatoes and prick all over with a toothpick.
2. Mix the sherry, vodka, and cayenne in a screw-top jar with a lid and add salt and pepper.
3. Drop the cherry tomatoes into the jar and let them sink into the liquid. Seal. This recipe should make enough to fill two 1 pint jars. Let stand in a cool place for 3 days.
4. Open the jar and serve.

TIPS Try not to squash them, but nestle them in so they are all snug and no space is wasted.

FEEDS: A SMALL PARTY
PREPARATION TIME: 24–36 HOURS
COOKING TIME: 0 MINUTES
♥ ✓ WF DF GF Ve

FEEDS: 4
PREPARATION TIME: 5 MINUTES
COOKING TIME: 15 MINUTES

Henry's sweet and sour shrimp

—8 **shrimp**
1 small **fresh red chile**
1 inch piece of **fresh ginger**
3 tablespoons **rice vinegar**
2 tablespoons **honey**
1 teaspoon **vegetable oil**
a pinch of **sea salt**

1. Peel the shrimp but leave the tails on. Seed the chile and chop finely. Finely chop the ginger. Put the chile and ginger into a saucepan over low heat with the vinegar and honey, and simmer until the sauce has reduced to a coating consistency.
2. Cook the shrimp in the vegetable oil for about a minute and a half on each side (or cook them on a grill). Season well and drop into the sauce. Serve.

Henry on his 5th birthday, 1975

Jossy's quick cheese straws

Party savories recipe
5

Although these are made with whole-wheat flour, they are deliciously light.

5 oz **sharp cheddar** or other strong cheese
2 teaspoons **paprika**
¾ cup **whole-wheat flour**
2 teaspoons **baking powder**
1 stick **unsalted butter**
2 **egg yolks**

1. Preheat the oven to 425°F.
2. Shred the cheese and put into a mixing bowl. Mix the paprika into the flour and then into the cheese. Cut the butter into small pieces and rub into the flour and cheese with your fingertips. Add the baking powder.
3. Add the egg yolks and mix to a stiff dough with a wooden spoon.
4. Using floured hands, gather the dough into a ball and, on a floured board, press out with the palms of your hands until about ½ inch thick.
5. Cut into straws—they can be varying lengths, but should be about ¾ inch wide—and place on a large, ungreased baking sheet.
6. Bake the straws at the top of the oven for 8–12 minutes, until golden brown.

PREPARATION TIME: 20 MINUTES
COOKING TIME: 15 MINUTES (APPROX)
FEEDS 8–10

TIPS

You can vary the flavor of these by substituting mild curry powder, caraway seeds, or other spices for the paprika. The straws are irresistible while still slightly warm, but any that survive can be kept for several days in an airtight container.

Jossy, 1976

Kamal

Our friend Kamal lives in Beirut and knows how to throw a party. This menu is inspired by an evening we spent in Mounir—a huge restaurant on the hillside that overlooks the city—drinking arak and eating until we were stuffed.

You can make everything except the halloumi in advance.

This feast will serve 8 well. Great with ice cold arak (arak is never drunk from the refrigerator, it must be made cold with ice cubes).

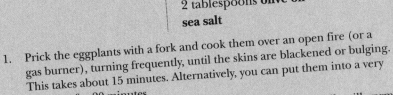

KAMAL'S EGGPLANT PUREE

Kamal is very particular about his moutabal, especially that it should not contain garlic. This is the best we have ever tasted. (If you make it with yogurt instead of tahini, it becomes babaganoush—in the Syrian way.)

Feeds: 4 as part of a mezze
Preparation time: 20 minutes
Cooking time: 0 minutes

2 large **eggplants**
½ cup **tahini**
juice of 3 **lemons**
2 tablespoons **olive oil**
sea salt

RECIPE TESTED BY JACKIE

1. Prick the eggplants with a fork and cook them over an open fire (or a gas burner), turning frequently, until the skins are blackened or bulging. This takes about 15 minutes. Alternatively, you can put them into a very hot oven for 20 minutes.

2. Peel off the blackened skin with a sharp knife, preferably while still warm, and either mash the inside with a fork or process in a food processor.

3. Add the tahini and lemon juice and season with salt.

4. Serve with a drizzle of olive oil.

GRILLED HALLOUMI

Squeaky cheese. We love it, and it has been a fixture on the Leon dinner menu since we opened.

Simply grill or broil sliced halloumi, Muenster, or mozzarella over low heat until turning a crispy brown (which should take 3 to 4 minutes), and serve with a squeeze of lemon.

You can add a mint, parsley, and a toasted seed topper to liven it up, if you desire.

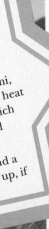

PARTY

TURKISH ALMOND DIP

You can cut any vegetables you like into sticks or pieces to eat with this nutty dip.

1 slice of good **white bread**, crusts removed
⅛ cup **unsalted almonds**, in their skins
1 large clove of **garlic**
2 tablespoons **lemon juice**
⅛ cup **extra virgin olive oil**
2 tablespoons **sunflower oil**
2 heaping tablespoons **plain yogurt**
a little **milk**

sea salt and **freshly ground black pepper**

1. Dip the bread into a bowl of water and squeeze dry.
2. Put the almonds into a food processor and process until they are as fine as possible.
3. Crush or grate the garlic and add to the processor, along with the soaked bread, lemon juice, both the oils, and the yogurt.
4. Process until smooth, adding a little milk if it seems too thick. Season with salt and pepper.
5. Spoon into a serving bowl and refrigerate for 30 minutes or more. Before serving with the prepared vegetables, trickle with a spoonful of olive oil.

RECIPE TESTED BY GEORGIE

Preparation time: 15 minutes Cooking time: 0 minutes

Preparation time: 5 minutes Cooking time: 5 minutes

HUMMUS TOPPER

Use store-bought hummus or the recipe from the first Leon cookbook and jazz it up with this meaty topper.

½ a **red bell pepper**
1 tablespoon **olive oil**
1 tablespoon **cumin seeds**
5 oz **ground lamb**
a squeeze of **lemon juice**
sea salt and **freshly ground black pepper**

1. Finely dice the red bell pepper.
2. In a skillet, heat the olive oil, add the bell pepper, and cook for a minute.
3. Add the cumin seeds and the ground lamb and season with salt and pepper.
4. Cook over high heat until the meat is crispy and cooked through.
5. Squeeze with some lemon juice, then scatter the lamb mixture over your hummus.

RECIPE TESTED BY TARQUIN

TZATSIKI

RECIPE TESTED BY LUCY

1 **cucumber**
½ a clove of **garlic**
a handful of **fresh mint**
1 cup **plain yogurt**
a squeeze of **lemon juice**
sea salt and **freshly ground black pepper**

1. Halve the cucumber lengthwise and scrape out the seeds, then grate. Scatter with salt and let stand for a few minutes, then squeeze out well and put into a large bowl.
2. Finely chop the garlic and mint. Add to the yogurt along with the cucumber, and stir well.
3. Season with salt and pepper, and add lemon juice to taste.

Parties have always been a big part of Leon life. The best kind are the ones where it gets to one in the morning and your granny is still on the dance floor and the kids are bouncing around her knees. No one does this like the Spanish. Any nation that starts going out for dinner at 10 p.m. has partying in its blood.

Everything can be made in advance, with the exception of the papas con chorizo. Serve it all with some chunks of good bread and olive oil for dipping.

This spread will serve 8 comfortably.

Papas con chorizo

A twist on the classic tapas dish, using sweet potatoes in place of potatoes..

Preparation time: 5 minutes
Cooking time: 35–40 minutes
✓ WF DF GF

6 raw **chorizo sausages**
3 large **sweet potatoes**
1 tablespoon **olive oil**
1 tablespoon **fennel seeds**
1 tablespoon **dried red pepper flakes**
   (we like the less hot oily ones)
sea salt and **freshly ground black pepper**

1. Preheat the oven to 350°F.
   Cut the chorizo into horizontal slices.
2. Peel the sweet potatoes and cut into ¾ inch cubes.
   Put into a large baking pan. Add the olive oil, fennel seeds, red pepper flakes, and seasoning, and mix thoroughly with your hands.
3. Put into the oven. After 20 minutes, add the chorizo to the pan and cook for another 15 minutes.

Rosemary Toasted Almonds

This is our friend Claire's recipe and is a fixture on the Leon dinner menu.

Preparation time: 2 minutes
Cooking time: 10 minutes
♥ ✓ WF DF GF V

3½ cups **whole almonds**, with skins
6 sprigs of **fresh rosemary**
3 tablespoons **extra virgin olive oil**
sea salt

1. Preheat the oven to 325°F.
2. Spread the almonds out evenly on a baking sheet (no more than 3 layers deep). Add 4 of the rosemary sprigs. Remove the leaves from the remaining sprigs and set aside.
3. Toast in the oven for about 7 minutes, or until just starting to go brown.
4. While still hot, toss with the olive oil and salt. Remove and discard the rosemary sprigs and add the reserved leaves. Return to the oven for another 3 minutes, until the almonds are fully toasted. Do not overtoast, or they will turn bitter.

Claire making an "experiment" cake, age of 5

Spanish Party

Manchego & Quince Jelly

This Spanish cheese is now available in good supermarkets and at many of the food markets that are springing up around the country. It has a supernatural affinity with quinces and ice-cold beer. You can serve it with store-bought membrillo (a kind of thick paste made from quinces) or with Petra's Quince Jelly on page 261.

Boquerones (Pickled Anchovies)

You can now buy these from most supermarkets. It is important to get the pickled ones—not the salted ones, or the ones in cans. Simply drizzle them with good olive oil and sprinkle with coarsely chopped parsley. Serve with toothpicks to skewer them into the mouth.

SLOW
FAST
FOOD

This section is about dishes that you can cook in advance and whip out speedily when you want them.

While these recipes may take a little longer to cook, we have done our best to make sure that they remain simple. Many of them are actually very quick to prepare, but need longer bubbling on the heat. Once cooked, they are wonderful reheated: ideal to put into the oven while you put your feet up with a glass of wine.

THE SCIENCE PART

> Briefly, either cook your meat hot and fast or long and gentle. Anything between is liable to end in toughness.

The next two sections—Slow Cooks and Pot Roasts—deal with food that needs to cook slowly so that the flavors mix, mellow, and mature. While there are some vegetarian recipes here, this is principally a style of cooking that is used for meat, which is where the science comes in.

Meat is made up of juicy muscle cells and connecting fibers. The connecting fibers are made principally of collagen, which is tough. To make your meat tender and delicious, you have three options:

Option 1

Buy more expensive cuts of meat (which tend not to have much connecting fiber) and cook them quickly. The juicy muscle cells stay intact and retain their moisture. The result is a succulent morsel—think good steak, pink lamb chops, or grilled chicken breast.

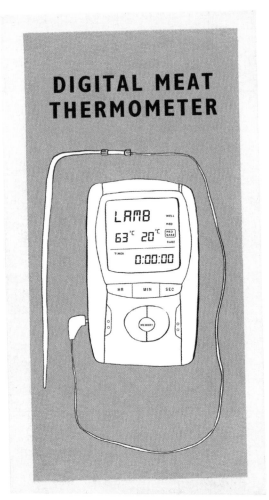

DIGITAL MEAT THERMOMETER

If you cook the meat for a little too long, however, the muscle cells start to break and lose their moisture and the meat gets tough. This happens at different temperatures for different meats. Using a meat thermometer, with the probe inside the thickest part of the cut (for poultry, the thickest part of the thigh, can guarantee that you get it right every time.

INTERNAL TEMPERATURES FOR PERFECTLY COOKED
MEAT

BEEF
Roasts . . . . .145°F
Steaks . . . . .145°F
Ground beef . . . . . . .160°F
Burgers) . . . . .160°F

LAMB
Roasts . . . . .145°F
Chops . . . . .145°F
Ground lamb . . . . . . .160°F

CHICKEN (and other poultry)
Whole bird . . . . .160°F

PORK
Roasts . . . . .145°F
Chops . . . . .145°F

Option 2

Take a cheaper cut of meat, with more tough connecting tissue, and cook it for longer. This is the method most often used in the following pages. As they pass the temperatures in the table above, the muscle cells burst, releasing their moisture (which initially makes the meat turn tough). Prolonged cooking in liquid, however, leads to the breaking down of the collagen and the reabsorption of the liquid, creating the familiar soft flavors and textures of braised meat.

The only way you can go wrong here is to get stuck between Option 1 and Option 2—muscle cells burst but collagen is still intact—in which case your meat will be tough. Don't worry: just put it back into the oven. It will only get better. (And you can add a little water, wine, or stock if the dish as a whole is drying out.)

Option 3

The invention of accurate meat thermometers and electric ovens that can hold temperatures consistently has led in recent years to a third way.

By happy scientific coincidence, collagen starts to break down at around 122°F but cell walls only start to burst (and lose their fluid) at around 140°F. Therefore, if you take the temperature of your meat up incredibly slowly and leave it at around 130°F for 10 hours or more, the collagen will dissolve while the cell walls stay intact. This means the final result will be unbelievably tender but also pink and juicy.

This is new-style slow cooking and has become fashionable in fancy restaurants, because the results can be mind-blowing. It is tricky to do, but deeply satisfying when you get it right. All you need is an oven that will hold an accurate—and sufficiently low—temperature, plus a meat thermometer. The only drawback of this method is that it doesn't make any juice for gravy.

HENRY'S 18-HOUR BEEF

A great dish to make when you want to go out on Saturday night, read the papers on Sunday morning, and still have 15 people around for Sunday dinner.

Saturday night 8 p.m. (if you do it a couple of hours earlier that would be fine, too):

1. Before you go out, set your oven to 140°F. Check that it is stable at this temperature by putting the meat probe in the oven and checking it after 10 minutes. If you can't get your oven to be stable at 140°F, you can't cook beef like this. Sorry. (With my oven, I have to tap the temperature gauge around a little to get it just right. A digital temperature setting would make things easier.)

2. Smear the outside of a good-size cut of beef (I like rib on the bone) with copious coarsely ground black pepper and Dijon or whole-grain mustard. Heat a roasting pan on the stove until very hot, add some oil and sear the beef so it turns a crisp, golden brown on all sides—the way you want it to look when you serve it up.

3. Put the probe thermometer into the center of the beef and put it, still in the roasting pan, into the 140°F oven.

4. Go out.

Saturday before you go to bed:

1. Check the thermometer (no need to open the oven)—if it is above 122°F already, it probably means your oven is too high. Take the probe out of the beef and leave it on the rack in the oven so that you can check the oven temperature. Once you are confident that the oven is at 140°F, put the probe back in and go to bed.

Sunday morning:

1. Turn the oven up to 150°F.

2. While you are reading the papers, check every half hour or so as the temperature rises. Very rare is 130°F. Medium 140°F. I think it is perfect at 136°F. The temperatures rise very slowly, so it is easy to hit the required one. Once the meat is done—this should be around 1 p.m.—set the oven to the same temperature (i.e. if you want it very rare, set it to 130°F). The meat will just sit at that temperature now, getting more and more tender. You can leave it as long as necessary without worrying (in fact, you could eat it for dinner if you wanted—it will only get more tender).

Sunday 2 p.m. (or 3 p.m. or 4 p.m. or 5 p.m. or whenever):

1. Pull out the beef. No need to rest it. Just carve it when you are ready.

GRAVY

As the beef doesn't produce any juice when you cook it this way, you will have to make gravy from a previously made stock. Or alternatively, serve it as I normally do, with a béarnaise and/or some creamy horseradish. (For fresh horseradish sauce, grate the root and mix it with lightly whipped cream or plain yogurt, vinegar, English mustard, salt, and pepper.)

215

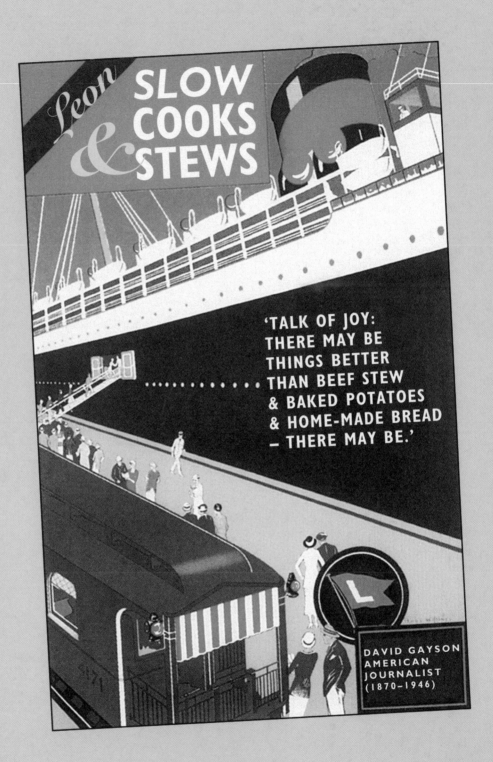

Leon

SLOW COOKS & STEWS

'TALK OF JOY:
THERE MAY BE
THINGS BETTER
THAN BEEF STEW
& BAKED POTATOES
& HOME-MADE BREAD
– THERE MAY BE.'

DAVID GAYSON
AMERICAN
JOURNALIST
(1870–1946)

LEON CHILI CON CARNE

A classic chili, now a fixture on the Leon menu—a great dish to prepare in advance and freeze.

Feeds: 6–8
Preparation time: 10 minutes
Cooking time: 2 hours
✓ WF DF GF

3 **carrots**
2 **onions**
4 cloves of **garlic**
2 sticks of **celery**
3 tablespoons **olive oil**
2¼ lb **ground beef**
3 **bay leaves**
2 teaspoons **ground cumin**
1 teaspoons **oregano**
⅛ cup **tomato paste**
3 (14½ oz) cans of **diced tomatoes**
2 teaspoons **smoked sweet paprika**
3 teaspoons **cayenne pepper**
½ cup **malt vinegar**
2 (15 oz) cans of **kidney beans**, drained and rinsed
sea salt and **freshly ground black pepper**

1. Peel and quarter the carrots and onions and put in a food processor. Peel the garlic and add it along with the celery, then process until they are all very finely chopped.

2. Heat the oil in a large saucepan and add the processed vegetables. Sauté over gentle heat until the vegetables have softened.

3. Add the ground beef and cook for 10 minutes, or until it is brown all over. Then add the rest of the ingredients and stir well. Cook for 2 hours on the stove, uncovered, stirring now and then. Add a little water, if necessary, to prevent it from drying out.

Henry and Mima

FRIENDS & FAMILY RECIPES

We'd been working on a classic chili dish for a while when my wife Mima by coincidence cooked me this one at home. Quest ended. It went straight on the menu.
Henry

Clockwise from top left: Leon Chili Con Carne; Benny's Slow Cooked Lamb; Chicken with Green Olives & Preserved Lemons

BENNY'S SLOW-COOKED LAMB
with kohlrabi & Indian spices

Kohlrabi is becoming increasingly available, and is great for slow-cooked dishes because it keeps its shape (pictured on page 218).

Feeds: 4
Preparation time: 20 minutes
Cooking time: 4 hours
✓ WF GF

1 **shoulder of lamb** (about 1¾ lb)
4 **onions**
3 **kohlrabi** (about 3¼ lb)
a 1¼ inch piece of **fresh ginger**
¼ cup **canola oil**
1 cup **plain yogurt**
2 tablespoons **medium curry powder**
1 teaspoon **garam masala**
a handful of toasted slivered **almonds**
sea salt and **freshly ground black pepper**

1. Preheat the oven to 300°F. Cut the lamb into 2 inch cubes. Cut the onions into thin rings. Peel and dice the kohlrabi. Finely chop the ginger.

2. Heat the oil in a heavy flameproof casserole dish over medium heat. Add the onions and a sprinkling of salt and cook for 15 minutes, or until caramelized and brown.

3. Add the lamb and ginger. Season and stir. Reduce the heat to low, add the yogurt, and bring to a boil.

4. Add the curry powder and stir for a minute or so. Pour in about 4 cups of water, or enough to cover the lamb comfortably, then add the kohlrabi and bring to a gentle simmer.

5. Cover with a lid, place in the oven, and cook for 3 hours, stirring every hour or so.

6. Stir in the garam masala and check the seasoning, then sprinkle the toasted almonds over the curry and serve.

TIPS

o Serve with basmati rice (see recipe on page 86) or other long-grain rice.

Little Benny, 1983

FRIENDS & FAMILY RECIPES

CHICKEN WITH GREEN OLIVES & PRESERVED LEMONS

A tangy Moroccan dish and a regular summer dish on the Leon menu (pictured on page 218).

Feeds: 4
Preparation time: 15 minutes
Cooking time: 30 minutes
✓ WF GF

1 **onion**
2 tablespoons **extra virgin olive oil**
2 cloves of **garlic**
½ teaspoon **ground ginger**
1 teaspoon **ground cumin**
10½ oz **skinless chicken thighs**, on the bone
2 cups **chicken stock**
a strand of **saffron**
1 cup of drained and rinsed canned **chickpeas**
2¼ oz **preserved lemon rinds**
½ cup **pitted green olives**
a small handful of **fresh cilantro**
2 tablespoons **crème fraîche** or **Greek yogurt**
sea salt and **freshly ground black pepper**

1. Peel and slice the onions and sauté them in the oil in a large saucepan or flameproof casserole dish for a couple of minutes until just soft. Smash and chop the garlic cloves (don't bother to peel them) and add them to the pan with the ground ginger and cumin. Sauté for a few more minutes.

2. Add the chicken thighs, stock, saffron, and chickpeas and simmer gently for 10 minutes.

3. Meanwhile, slice the preserved lemon rinds and halve the olives. Add these to the pan and simmer gently for 5 minutes. Coarsely chop the cilantro.

4. Add the crème fraîche and cilantro and turn the heat up slightly for another 5 minutes to reduce the sauce. Adjust the seasoning and serve.

TIPS

○ You can use leftover chicken from a roast—just add it toward the end of cooking

FRIENDS & FAMILY RECIPES

A gang of us went to Marrakech for the weekend for Greg's 40th, where those who were eager did a day's cooking course at the wonderful Maison Arabe. We cooked this dish, then all sat around the beautiful pool and ate our offerings in the North African sun—heaven!
Apple

Apple and Sophie in Morocco, 2001

My wife Katie
is very tolerant about putting up
with my nutritional and health
adventures. After I suggested we
might try to eat less red meat,
she was a little concerned about how
to satisfy our love of bolognaise…
until her friend Robin the weather
man suggested that we use turkey
instead, saying "you'd never know
the difference." And he is right.
Well done Robin.
And thank you Katie.
John

Feeds: 6   Preparation time: 10 minutes   Cooking time: 1½–2 hours   ✓ DF

TURKEY BOLOGNESE

A great way to use up leftover turkey, and terrific if you are trying to cut back on red meat.

Katie and Natasha in ... Turkey

RECIPE TESTED BY: JULIA

2 **onions**
2 cloves of **garlic**
3½ cups **mushrooms**
2 tablespoons **olive oil**
1¼ lb **ground turkey**
1 **dried chile**
2 (14½ oz) cans of **diced tomatoes**
2 tablespoons **tomato paste**
1⅛ cups **red wine**
2 cups **chicken stock**
a dash of **Worcestershire sauce**
a large sprig of **fresh thyme**
sea salt and **freshly ground black pepper**

1. Peel and finely chop the onions and garlic, and slice the mushrooms.

2. Heat the olive oil in a saucepan, add the onions and garlic, and cook until they are starting to brown. Add the ground turkey and brown it all over, stirring to make sure it's cooked throughout.

3. Crumble in the chile, add the mushrooms, season, and cook for a few minutes.

4. Add the diced tomatoes, tomato paste, wine, chicken stock, Worcestershire sauce, and thyme.

5. Simmer gently on the stove with the lid on for a good hour and a half, making sure it doesn't boil.

TIPS

o   If you are using leftover turkey, grind it into ground in a food processor and add it together with the chile in step 3.

o   If the bolognese seems to be drying out, add more chicken stock, if you have it, or water.

o   After simmering on the stove initially, you can transfer it to an ovenproof dish and cook it in a low oven for an hour, at around 300°F.

Feeds: 4 (with pasta)   Preparation time: 15 minutes   Cooking time: 2–3 hours   ✓ WF DF GF

BEST BOLOGNESE

No freezer should be without a few bags of bolognese. This simple meat sauce recipe for pasta is given real depth of flavor thanks to long cooking and a touch of cinnamon.

3 tablespoons **olive oil**
2 **onions**
4 cloves of **garlic**
8 oz **streaky bacon** (as fatty as you can find)
2¼ lb **ground beef**
1 (14½ oz) can of **diced tomatoes**
½ teaspoon **ground cinnamon**
2 tablespoons **tomato paste**
2 cups **red wine**

1. Heat the oil in a largish saucepan. Finely chop the onions and garlic and add to the pan. Let soften for 2 minutes.

2. Chop the bacon into small pieces and add to the pan.

3. When the bacon is starting to turn brown at the edges, add the beef and stir to break it up so that it browns all over.

4. Add the canned tomatoes, cinnamon, tomato paste, and red wine.

5. Stir, then put a lid on and let simmer for 2–3 hours, adding water, if necessary, to prevent it from drying out.

TIPS

o   If I have this on spaghetti, I prefer it with grated cheddar instead of Parmesan. It reminds me of my 1970s childhood.

o   This is a very versatile dish. Use it to make lasagna. Or stuff zucchini or tomatoes with it and bake in a hot oven for 20 minutes. Slice some potatoes, lay them on top, and bake for 30 minutes.

o   The long cooking time is essential to give this dish real depth. Resist the temptation to shorten it too much.

RECIPE TESTED BY: BEN

o   A great dish to make in batches of up to four times this amount. Freeze in single portions in small freezer bags.

GILES'S CHOLENT

Henry's friend Giles made this classic Jewish dish a regular weekend feature when his tepid oven only allowed for long slow cooks.

Feeds: 6
Preparation time: 20 minutes
+ soaking time
Cooking time: 12 hours +
✓ WF DF

1 **beef brisket** (about 3¼ lb)
2 tablespoons **olive oil**
2 large **onions**
6 cloves of **garlic**
1 cup **pearl barley**
1 tablespoon Hungarian **paprika**
1⅛ cups **dried navy beans** (soaked in water for a few hours, then drained and rinsed)
4 cups of **fresh beef stock**
sea salt and **freshly ground black pepper**

1. In a medium, flameproof casserole dish, brown the rolled brisket in olive oil, then remove it from the pan and put it aside.

2. Peel and coarsely slice the onions. Peel the garlic but keep the cloves whole. Put them into the dish and sauté until they smell nice.

3. Add the pearl barley and paprika and sauté for a minute or two, adding a splash of oil if it all looks stupidly dry.

4. Add the dried navy beans (soaked for a couple of hours). Stir it all about, put the brisket back in, and add the beef stock and enough water to cover. Season with salt and pepper.

5. Use a piece of aluminum foil under the lid to make a hermetic seal, and place the casserole dish in the oven at around 200°F (or lower) for around 12 hours. Put it in at around midnight and you'll be on time for lunch.

6. Remove the lid at the table and you should find the beans and barley cooked (maybe a bit crunchy at the top if there wasn't enough water, though these parts can be stirred in to lend "complexity"), and the top third of the brisket poking out like a tiny hippo in a swamp, the fat all yellow and yummy-looking. Application of a fork and spoon should pull the meat apart easily.

TIPS

○ Serve up the cholent with plenty of beans and barley and have a jar of pickled cucumbers on the table.

○ Always use Hungarian paprika instead of Spanish, because it retains its red color and doesn't turn brown.

With biblical prohibitions against fire-kindling on the Sabbath, Jewish mothers in the shtetl used to make this dish on Friday before sunset and deliver it to the baker, where it cooked slowly overnight in a warm oven, to be picked up by the husband and children on the way back from shul in the morning. I, however, began cooking it when staying in a cottage in Hawkshead in the Lake District—capital of Wordsworth country—whose only stove was a not very good Aga that never got much hotter than a construction worker's armpit. I made cholent most weekends, and afterwards would stroll down to the actual synagogue where Wordsworth was barmitzvah'd in 1783. *Giles*

FRIENDS & FAMILY
RECIPES

Giles with his sister Victoria, 1975

BRUNO'S OSSO BUCCO

This is a version of the Italian classic, simplified from a recipe by Henry's old boss, chef Bruno Loubet—it's a great party piece to serve if you have friends coming around. (It is fine to eat certified-humane, preferably pasture-raised veal, because it comes from the male cows in dairy herds that would otherwise go to waste.)

Feeds: 6
Preparation time: 10 minutes
Cooking time: 2¼ hours
✓ WF DF GF

2 **carrots**
1 **onion**
1 stick of **celery**
2 cloves of **garlic**
3 tablespoons **vegetable oil**
6 slices of **certified-humane veal shank**
1 bottle of **white wine**
4 **plum tomatoes**
8 medium-large **fresh sage leaves**
2 large strips of **orange zest**
sea salt and **freshly ground black pepper**

1. Peel and finely chop the carrots, onions, celery, and garlic.

2. Heat the oil in a flameproof casserole dish over high heat and brown the meat well on both sides (you will need to do this in two or three batches).

3. Remove the meat from the dish, lower the heat, then add the vegetables and let them color. Add the meat back to the dish then add the wine.

4. Chop the tomatoes and add them to the dish with the sage and 1 strip of orange zest. Cook over very low heat for 2 hours, or until the meat is falling off the bone.

5. At this point you can refrigerate the whole thing for up to a week.

6. Remove the meat and vegetables and strain the sauce into a small saucepan and heat to reduce until lovely and thick. Either plate up the meat and veg and pour the sauce over them, or return the meat to the casserole dish, add the sauce, and serve in the pot. Finely chop the remaining strip of orange zest and sprinkle on top for the final touch. You could add chopped parsley too, if you desire.

TIPS

o The vegetables will be well cooked after the 2 hours are up, so some people sauté a few more carrots and add them at the end to give a little bite.

o The Italians traditionally serve this with saffron risotto (*risotto Milanese*) and gremolata (chopped parsley, garlic, and lemon zest), but it also goes well with mashed potatoes, grits or tagliatelle.

o Serve with a green salad on the side and a good red wine.

FRIENDS & FAMILY
RECIPES

POT ROASTS

Pot roasting seems too easy to be true. Just put everything into a pot and put the pot into the oven.

The opportunities for experimentation are legion. This section contains a few pot-roasting recipes to get you going, but once you get into the habit, you'll find yourself making up new versions all the time. Here are a few tips to help you get the right balance of flavors.

1. What is your theme?
It's a good idea to build your experiments on classic dishes. Classics are classics for a reason—they are combinations that work together well and have been improved upon over the years that they have been handed down. So whether it's a beery English stew or a fruity Moroccan tagine or stew, decide on your theme.

2. How are you going to cook the meat?
There are two things to consider. First, how are you going to brown it? You can do this beforehand by frying it in the pot, or at the end by taking the lid off. Either way, you don't want to miss resulting flavors. Second, are you going to cook it so that it is plump and firm or so it is falling apart? (See Slow Cooking: The Science Part, page 212.)

3. What is the architecture of the dish?
Think about what vegetables you are going to use and how you are going to chop them. It makes a big difference to the finished result if everything isn't just chopped the same. Also, resist the temptation to throw in too many different vegetables. Keep it simple.

4. What flavors are you going to add to the meat and vegetables?
This could be herbs or spices at the start, or something flavorsome stirred in at the end to perk it up (see the Winter Vegetable Herb Pot Roast on page 241). Be bold.

5. What is providing the sweetness? What is providing the sour?
All great dishes have a balance of sweet and sour. These could come from numerous sources. Good sweeteners include carrots, slow-cooked garlic or onions; dried fruit, such as apricots or prunes; beer, squash or sweet potatoes, or simply honey. You can add the sour with vinegar; alcohol such as wine, beer, sherry, or brandy; citrus or other acidic fruit; tamarind, verjuice (unripened grape juice); and amchoor (a dried powder made from unripe mangoes).

CHICKEN POT ROAST

This is the classic simple dinner—put it all into a large pot or dutch oven when you get home and spend your evening doing something you enjoy.

Feeds: 4
Preparation time: 15 minutes
Cooking time: 1½–2 hours
WF GF DF

5 slices of **bacon**
8 **carrots** (about 1 lb)
4 **Yukon gold** or **white round potatoes**
3 **onions**
1 whole bulb of **garlic**
6 sprigs of **fresh thyme**
2 tablespoons **extra virgin olive oil**
1¼ cups **white wine**
1 whole **chicken** (about 3¼–4½ lb)
sea salt and **freshly ground black pepper**

1. Heat the oven to 375°F.

2. Coarsely chop the bacon. Peel the carrots, but leave the potatoes and onions unpeeled. Coarsely chop the carrots and potatoes, and cut the onions into quarters. Cut the unpeeled garlic bulb in half across the middle. Place all these into a casserole dish with the thyme and seasoning. Add 1 tablespoon of the olive oil and toss thoroughly. Pour in the white wine.

3. Rub the chicken with the remaining tablespoon of olive oil and season well. Place on top of the vegetables.

4. Cook for 1 hour, covered, then remove the lid and cook for 30 minutes to 1 hour, depending on its size, to brown the chicken and make sure it is cooked through.

TIPS

○ This dish is very versatile. Almost any mixture of vegetables, herbs, and spices will work as the base. Try thinking in themes: winter pot roast—using root vegetables and sage; German pot roast—using cabbage, some pieces of sausage, and juniper.

○ You don't need to use chicken. You can use this method with almost any meat—game, beef (particularly the cheap cuts), or lamb. For tougher meats, you may need to use more liquid and cook for longer.

○ Experiment with the liquid: vermouth, stock, and beer all work well.

○ If you want something lower GI, replace the potatoes with sweet potatoes.

○ If you don't use potatoes, this goes very well with tagliatelle. The combination of the juice and simple buttered pasta is one of life's great pleasures.

○ For added zing, blend a handful of soft green herbs, such as parsley, 1 tablespoon of olive oil, and 1 clove of garlic to a paste. Stir into the vegetables just before serving.

○ Try stirring a raw egg yolk into the sauce at the end of cooking to thicken it.

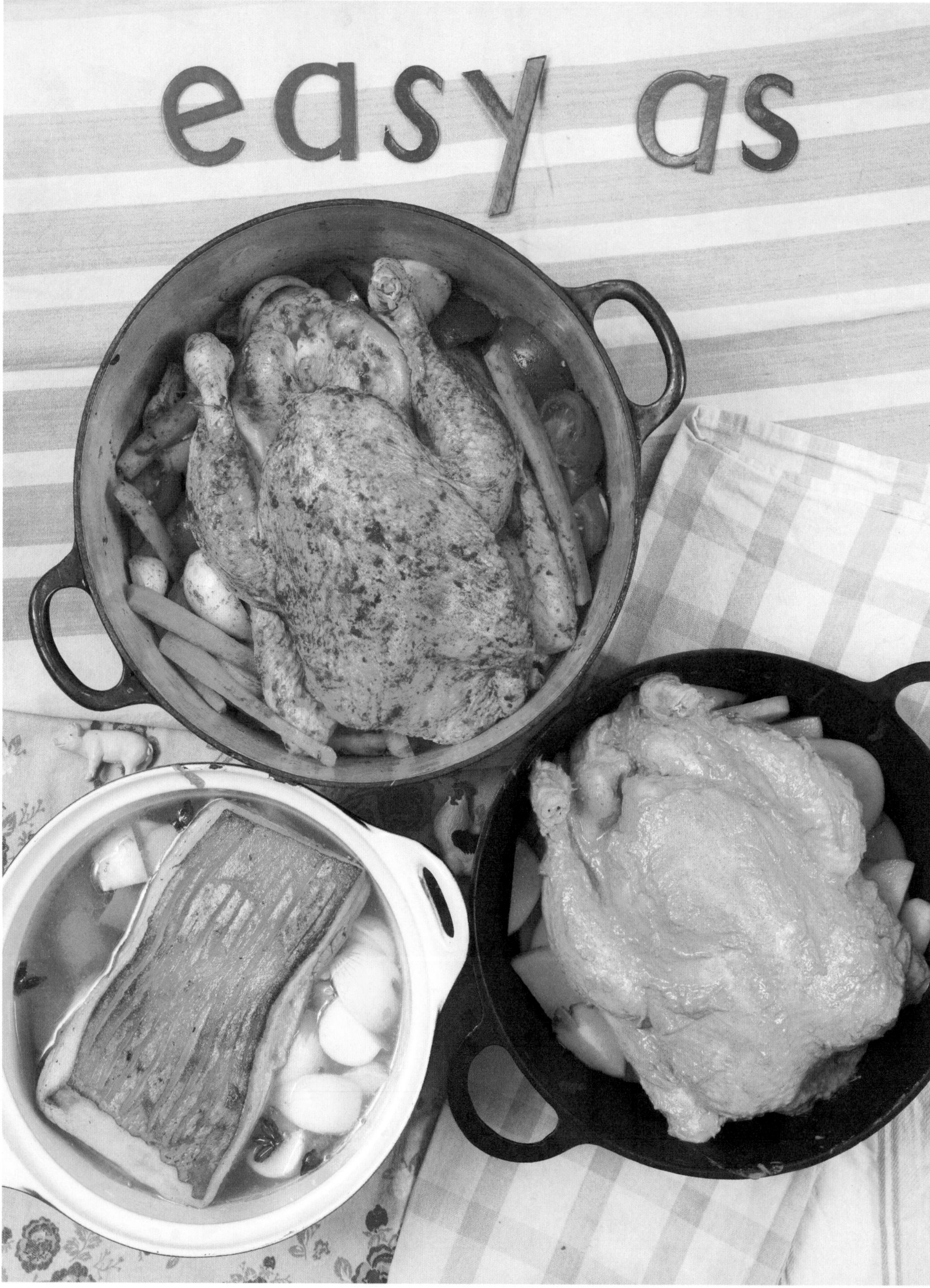
easy as

SPANISH POT ROAST

Warm and spicy.

Feeds: 4
Preparation time: 15 minutes
Cooking time: 1½–2 hours
✓ WF DF GF

3 **onions**
3 **carrots**
1 whole bulb of **garlic**
4 **tomatoes**
3 teaspoons **fennel seeds**
2 heaping teaspoons **smoked sweet paprika**
2 tablespoons **olive oil**
1 whole **chicken** (about 3¼–4½ lb)
2 tablespoons **sherry vinegar**
1 cup **white wine**
sea salt and **freshly ground black pepper**

1. Heat the oven to 375°F.

2. Quarter the onions (no need to peel them). Cut the carrots into long batons. Slice the bulb of garlic across and quarter the tomatoes.

3. Put all the vegetables in the bottom of a large casserole dish with the fennel seeds, 1 tablespoon of the olive oil, and 1 teaspoon of the paprika. Season well and stir.

4. Rub the remaining oil and paprika into the chicken along with some salt and pepper. Place the chicken on top of the vegetables and pour in the vinegar and white wine.

5. Cook in the oven for 1 hour, covered, then remove the lid and cook for another 30 minutes to 1 hour, depending on its size, to brown the chicken and make sure it is cooked through.

TIPS

○ Add some peeled potato chunks to the pot for a full meal in one pot.

○ Otherwise serve with rice or pasta.

○ If you like some spice, use hot paprika in place of the sweet stuff.

○ Great with some added chunks of chorizo mixed in with the vegetables.

RECIPE TESTED BY SAM & LILY

Clockwise from the top (all uncooked): Spanish Pot Roast; Indian Pot Roast Chicken; Pork Belly with Turnips & Prunes

INDIAN POT ROAST CHICKEN

The potatoes in this dish pick up a wonderful lemony, curried flavor (pictured on page 232).

Feeds: 4–6
Preparation time: 15 minutes
Cooking time: 1½–2 hours

WF GF

3 cloves of **garlic**
¼ cup **plain yogurt**
2 teaspoons **turmeric**
2 teaspoons **ground cinnamon**
2 teaspoons **ground coriander**
1 teaspoon **chili powder**
1½ lb **new potatoes**
1 teaspoon **vegetable oil**
1 **lemon**
1 whole **chicken** (about 3¼–4½ lb)
a handful of **fresh cilantro leaves**
sea salt and **freshly ground black pepper**

1. Preheat the oven to 375°F.

2. Peel and grate the garlic into a bowl, add the yogurt, spices, and chili and mix well.

3. Slice the unpeeled potatoes fairly thinly and place in a large casserole dish with the oil. Halve the lemon and slice one half finely. Add the lemon slices to the potatoes. Season with salt and pepper.

4. Smear the yogurt mixture all over the chicken and place it on top of the potatoes. Put the other half of the lemon inside the cavity of the bird.

5. Cook, covered, in the oven for 1 hour, then remove the lid and cook for another 30 minutes to 1 hour, depending on its size, to brown the chicken and make sure it is cooked through.

6. Remove the chicken from the casserole dish and place on a board. Put the potatoes into a serving dish and sprinkle with the cilantro leaves.

 TIPS

- If you don't have the spices, you could use a curry paste or powder in their place.

- Also good is to replace the spices with a tablespoon of lime pickle blended finely with the yogurt.

- To help the yogurt and spice mixture to permeate the chicken more, pull the skin away from the breast gently and spread some of the yogurt underneath the skin.

- Serve with a salad or simple green vegetables.

INDIAN POT ROAST CHICKEN

PORK BELLY WITH TURNIPS AND PRUNES

This dish is simple to make and full of flavor (pictured on page 232).

Feeds: 4
Preparation time: 10 minutes
Cooking time: 3 hours
✓ WF DF GF

a chunk of **pork belly** that fits into your casserole dish,
(about 2¼–3¼ lb) in weight
2 tablespoons **olive oil**
1 **turnip**
2 large **carrots**
1 large **onion**
10 **pitted prunes (dried plums)**
4 **star anise**
15 **coriander seeds**
1 bottle of **white wine** (it's worth it)
sea salt and **freshly ground black pepper**

1. Preheat the oven to 350°F.

2. Season the skin of the pork well, then brown it in the olive oil in your casserole dish. Remove the pork and set aside.

3. Peel the turnip and slice into ¼ inch circles. Peel the carrots and cut into batons. Peel and coarsely chop the onion. Halve the prunes. Add all the vegetables to the casserole dish with the prunes and spices.

4. Add the wine, then return the pork to the casserole dish and put the lid on.

5. Cook for 2½ hours (at least), until the meat is very tender—basting every 30 minutes and adding water if the vegetables dry out too much.

6. Remove the lid and cook for another 30 minutes.

TIPS

o The vegetables should end up as a glossy thick mixture at the end of cooking.

o You can carefully cut the skin off the pork and roast it in the oven at 400°F for 15 minutes to make it crispy, while the pork stays in the casserole dish.

o If you think the wine is a little extravagant, you can always replace most of it with chicken stock.

CHICKEN WITH 100 CLOVES OF GARLIC

A pot roast to show off with, and so simple; the garlic warms and softens and sweetens, and it creates a wonderful depth of flavor.

Feeds: 6
Preparation time: 10 minutes
Cooking time: 1½ hours
✓ WF GF DF

1 medium-size **chicken**, (about 2¼–3¼ lb)
a glug of **extra virgin olive oil**
3 large handfuls of **fresh thyme**
100 cloves of **garlic** (about 12 bulbs)
1 cup **red wine vinegar**
sea salt and **freshly ground black pepper**

1. Preheat the oven to 350°F.

2. Smear the chicken with olive oil and plenty of salt and pepper. Break up the garlic bulbs into cloves, but do not peel them.

3. Stuff the chicken with the thyme and about 20 cloves of garlic. Place the rest of the garlic in a casserole dish and nestle the chicken on top. Pour in the vinegar.

4. Cover and cook for approximately 1 hour, adding up to 1 cup of water if necessary to stop it from drying out.

5. Remove the lid and cook for another 30 minutes to brown the chicken.

TIPS

o   Serve with tagliatelle and a green salad with balsamic dressing (see page 163).

o   Try squeezing the roasted garlic from its skin and spreading it on bread with a little salt—a delicious way to use up the leftover garlic.

When John and I came to write our list of recipes for the book, this dish was on both our lists. This dish is a good example of how recipes are passed down through the generations. When I showed the recipe to my mom, she told me that it was a dish that her mother used to make, but in the old French tradition with 100 bulbs (rather than cloves) of garlic. That must have been something.
Henry

This has big memories for me. It is the first thing I ever cooked—for a girlfriend when I was fourteen. The recipe was given to me by my Auntie Nita. In retrospect, not a good dinner for a date …
John

Leon, Nita, Tim, Marion and Joe in Portugal 1965

RIGAS'S LAMB

This dish was made for us by our (Greek) friend Dimitri, from a recipe that has been handed down in his family for generations.

Rigas (left) with Chloe, Dimitri and Dan, Antiparos, Cyclades

Feeds: 6–8
Preparation time: 20 minutes
Cooking time: 3½ hours
DF

1 **leg of lamb**, on the bone
5 cloves of **garlic**
a small bunch of **fresh mint**
2 **onions**
2 (14½ oz) cans of **diced tomatoes**
⅓ cup **extra virgin olive oil**
12 oz **risoni**, **kritharaki**, or **small macaroni**
2 tablespoons **dried mint**
sea salt and **freshly ground black pepper**

1. Preheat the oven to 300°F.

2. With the tip of a sharp knife, make 6 or 7 deep holes on both sides of the meat. Stuff these with small pieces of garlic, followed by an equal amount of salt and black pepper mixed together. Plug the holes with a couple of leaves of fresh mint, and season the meat with a little more salt and pepper.

3. Finely chop the onions and put them into a large roasting dish. Add the tomatoes and oil and stir well. Put the meat on top, and place in the oven.

4. Cook for 3½ hours. Keep adding water to the sauce to prevent it from drying out. If you like, you can baste the lamb with spoonfuls of the sauce so that it forms a crust of caramelized onions on the meat.

5. When 20 minutes of cooking time is left, add a cup of water to the sauce and stir in the risoni or macaroni.

6. Season, sprinkle well with dried mint (use more than you think you should—it adds a peppery kick to the sauce), and put back into the oven until the pasta is tender. The risoni will expand and absorb the liquid sauce, which in turn will have absorbed all the juices from the meat. Keep adding water and stirring every 5–10 minutes, if needed to so that the pasta stays moist and doesn't stick.

TIPS

o To serve, try green beans, cooled slightly and sprinkled with lemon juice, olive oil, and salt and pepper. Otherwise a green or Greek salad makes a good accompaniment.

Rigas is my dad. Dad and his parents came to Britain as refugees from the Greek civil war in the forties. This recipe comes originally from his mom Vivi, who died while he was just a young man. On the little Greek island where dad's family house is still located, most people did not have gas ovens in their homes when I was a kid. My early memories of being there are of watching families walking through the village on Sundays with huge trays of lamb, pork, or stuffed tomatoes carried aloft; they were all heading to the bakery that had the only big ovens on the island, and which became a communal kitchen every weekend and feast day. Cooking this dish at home in London brings to mind whitewashed houses with blue shutters, the sound of crickets beating in the heat, and the strange sweet drinks that came out of a dispenser in the bakery. *Dimitri*

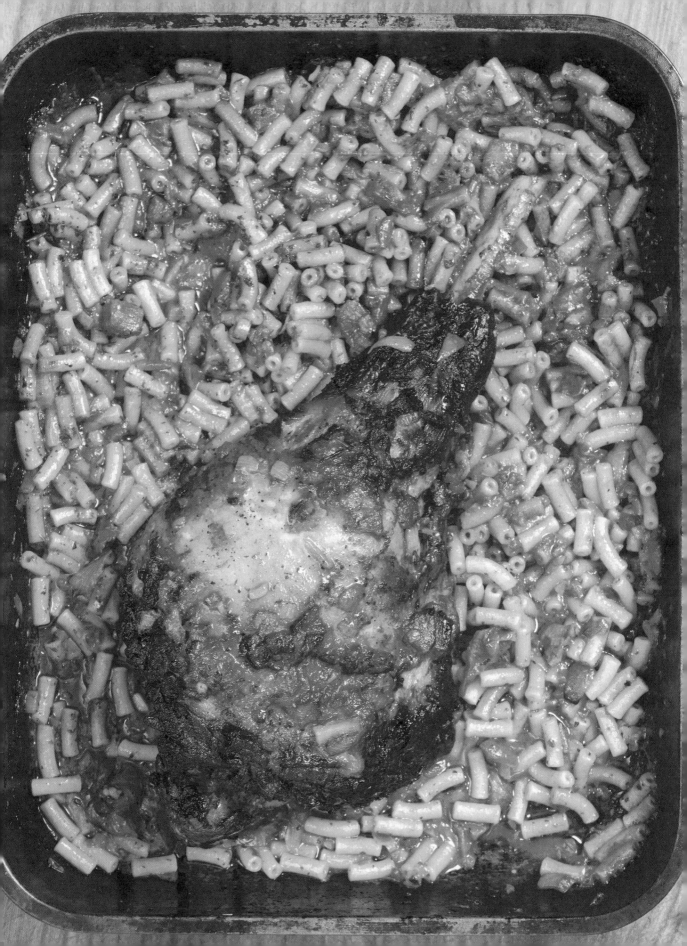

WINTER VEGETABLE HERB POT ROAST

A great way to use up ungainly winter vegetables. The trick is the flash of raw garlic and parsely at the end, which lifts everything.

Feeds: 4–6
Preparation time: 15 minutes
Cooking time: 1½ hours
♥ ✓ WF DF GF V

For the pot
2 **onions**
4 **parsnips**
1 **butternut squash**
3 **carrots**
a large handful of **fresh sage**
2 tablespoons **extra virgin olive oil**
1 glass of **white wine**
15 oz can of **great Northern beans**
sea salt and **freshly ground black pepper**

To finish
3 cloves of **garlic**
a handful of **fresh flat-leaf parsley**
a dash of **olive oil**

1. Preheat the oven to 400°F.

2. Peel and slice the onions. Peel the parsnips and quarter them lengthwise. Seed the butternut squash and cut it into large chunks (leaving the skin on). Peel the carrots and slice them diagonally. Coarsely chop the sage.

3. Put all the vegetables, except the beans, into a casserole dish with the olive oil, white wine, and sage. Cook in the oven for 1 hour with the lid on.

4. Add the drained beans and cook for another 30 minutes with the lid off. You may want to add a little water if it gets too dry.

5. Just before serving, process the garlic with the parsley and a little olive oil. Season and stir into the casserole.

TIPS

○ You can use any combination of winter vegetables—celeriac, pumpkin, potatoes, shallots, celery, turnips, rutabaga, beets, all work well.

○ Don't be afraid to mix in a few greens—kale, cabbage, and collard will all go well in the pot.

○ Try adding in a few chestnuts.

BOIL OR BAKE IN THE BAG

The seventies. The decade of space-age convenience food. Tang, Cup O'Noodles, Jell-O. Suddenly, all our meals had to be freeze-dried and reconstituted, as if we had turned into a nation of astronauts.

And then there's boil-in-a-bag: A seventies invention that has turned into a culinary classic. Often used by Michelin-starred chefs these days, it is one of the easiest ways to speedily prepare a quick meal or an extravagant dinner party.

Clockwise from top: Sea Bass with Thai Spices; Quail with Thyme & Garlic; Mackerel with Rosemary & Beans, all before cooking

243

QUAIL *with thyme & garlic*

Feeds: 2, as a starter
Preparation time: 15 minutes
Cooking time: 1½ hours
✓ WF GF

2 **quails**
1 tablespoon **olive oil**
½ a small **onion**
3 cloves of **garlic**
2 tablespoons **butter**
1 large bunch of **fresh thyme**
⅛ cup **chicken stock** (made with ¼ of a bouillon cube
    if you don't have fresh stock)
¼ cup **brandy**
 juice of 1 **lemon**
sea salt and **freshly ground black pepper**

1. Preheat the oven to 350°F.

2. Season the quails well with salt and pepper. Heat the olive oil in a skillet and brown the quails, breast side down.

3. Cut two rectangles of aluminum foil large enough to encase the quails, lay them on top of each other, and place in a baking pan. Place the browned quails in the middle of the foil, with their legs interlocking.

4. Very finely dice the onion and garlic and sprinkle on top with the butter and thyme. Draw up the foil round each side and pour in the stock, brandy, and lemon juice.

5. Seal the foil up as tightly as you can and put into the oven for 2 hours.

6. When the time is up, carefully open the package. If the sauce is liquid, pour it into a small saucepan and boil it down until reduced. Serve the sauce with the quails.

TIPS

o Serve with celeriac boiled in milk until soft and processed with butter and nutmeg.

o If you can't find quails, this works just as well with chicken thighs on the bone.

o As with all "foiled' dishes, you can get them ready for the oven a day in advance.

MACKEREL *with rosemary & beans*

Feeds: 4
Preparation time: 15 minutes
Cooking time: 30 minutes
♥ ✓ WF GF DF

½ a bulb of **fennel**
1 **carrot**
½ a **red onion**
½ (15 oz) can of **great Navy beans**
olive oil
2 whole **mackerel** or 4 **mackerel fillets**
a big sprig of **fresh rosemary**
1 cup **white wine**
sea salt and **freshly ground black pepper**

1. Preheat the oven to 425°F.

2. Chop the fennel and carrot into very fine strips and slice the onion finely. The vegetables must all be cut thin or they will not cook. Drain and rinse the great Navy beans.

3. Tear off 2 pieces of aluminum foil big enough to enclose the mackerel, lay them on top of each other, and place in a baking pan. Oil the foil center with a little olive oil.

4. Lay the mackerel (skin side down if using fillets) on the foil. Sprinkle with the fennel, carrot, and onion, and add the rosemary.

5. Top with the beans, season, and draw up the foil around the sides, leaving a pouring vent in the middle at the top. Pour in the white wine, seal the package well, and place in the oven for 30 minutes.

 TIPS

○ Works well with any robust fish.

○ Cannellini, lima, and cranberry beans work as well as great Navy beans.

SEA BASS *with Thai spices*

Feeds: 2
Preparation time: 10 minutes
Cooking time: 20 minutes
♥ ✓ WF GF DF

1 teaspoon **sesame oil**
2 fillets of **sea bass**
a 1 inch piece of **fresh ginger**
1 clove of **garlic**
½ a **fresh red chile**
2 **scallions**
1 tablespoon **Thai fish sauce**
2 tablespoons **white wine**
1 tablespoon **soy sauce**

1. Preheat the oven to 220°C/425°F/gas mark 7.

2. Tear off 2 rectangles of aluminum foil big enough to encase the fish, lay them on top of each other, and place in a baking pan. Lightly oil the center of the foil with the oil.

3. Lay the fish fillets skin side down on the foil.

4. Peel the ginger and garlic. Seed the chile. Chop them all finely. Cut the scallions into long diagonals. Sprinkle the ginger, garlic, chile and scallions over the fish.

5. Draw up the foil around each side, pour in the fish sauce, wine, and soy sauce, and seal up the foil as tightly as you can. Put into the oven and cook for 20 minutes.

 TIPS

○ Great with basmati rice, long-grained rice or rice noodles. To make this a meal in a bag, add a handful of canned cannellini beans to the foil before you seal it up.

FRIDGE RAIDERS

Provider of the fastest food in the world: the fridge. There for us in the morning, when we get back from work, and in the middle of the night.

This section is about knowing what to feed your old friend so that it can feed you.

These recipes can sit a while without suffering from the cold. Some of them—chicken drumsticks, say—are so easy to buy that you might never have thought of making your own. But the recipes are simple and fun, your friends will be disproportionately impressed, and you can be confident that no chemicals have found their way into the finished product.

Henry's refrigerator, including Spicy Chicken Drumsticks, Ginger Chile Shrimp, Roasted Artichokes, and Scotch Eggs

GINGER & CHILE SHRIMP

Feeds: 2
Preparation time: 5 minutes
Cooking time: 5 minutes
♥ ✓ WF DF GF

1 fresh **red chile**
a 1 inch piece of **fresh ginger**
10 large raw peeled **shrimp**
1 tablespoon **extra virgin olive oil**
sea salt and **freshly ground black pepper**

This dish scores well on ease, theater, and flavor. Cook this when you want to be on a beach in India without having to leave the house. It's tempting to have one hot before leaving the rest to cool and wait for you in the refrigerator.
John

1. Seed the chile and peel the ginger. Slice them both into fine strips.

2. Pan-fry everything in the olive oil until the shrimp are cooked and turn pink.

3. Season with salt and pepper and serve.

 TIPS

○ If you want to cheat, buy cooked shrimp, already shelled, and flash fry them for 2 minutes to heat through. You can also use dried red pepper flakes or powder. It's still best to use fresh ginger, though.

○ Be careful to check on the provenance of your shrimp when you buy them. You can now get sustainable ones from the North Atlantic.

SPICY CHICKEN DRUMSTICKS

These could not be more simple. A perfect thing to store in the refrigerator to pick on when hunger strikes at strange times.

Feeds: 4
Preparation time: 3 minutes
Cooking time: 45 minutes
✓ WF GF DF

8 **chicken drumsticks**
1 tablespoon **extra virgin olive oil**
1 tablespoon **honey**
2 teaspoons **mild curry powder**
½ a **lemon**
sea salt and **freshly ground black pepper**

1. Preheat the oven to 475°F.

2. Lay a sheet of aluminum foil in a baking pan, leaving a little excess sticking up around the sides.

3. With a sharp knife, slash the sides of the chicken drumsticks—this will let the flavors seep in and the meat cook evenly.

4. Put the chicken in a bowl and add the oil, honey, and curry powder and mix well to coat the chicken. Then transfer the chicken to the baking pan and add some salt and pepper. Put into the oven for 45 minutes, turning the drumsticks every 15 minutes or so.

5. Take out of the oven, let cool for a few minutes, then douse with a squeeze of lemon.

MARION'S SCOTCH EGGS

Best hot from the pan, but also a great fridge raider.

Feeds: 6
Preparation time: 20 minutes
Cooking time: 15 minutes
✓ DF

6 **eggs**
1 lb **bulk sausage** or **sausage meat**
    removed from the casings
2 teaspoons **English mustard**
2 handfuls of **fresh bread crumbs**
¼ cup **vegetable oil**
sea salt and **freshly ground black pepper**

John and his mom, 1972

IMMEDIATE

My mom Marion (Leon's wife) is in my book the mistress of Scotch eggs. We would either eat them warm, (lovely), or take them to the Essex coast (Tollesbury) on weekend trips. I still don't know whether they are best eaten whole (in many bites, not all at once) or cut in half. The only solution is to have two—one whole, one cut in two. *John*

IMMEDIATE

1. Hard boil the eggs, then shell them and dry with paper towels.

2. Season the meat with salt and pepper and add the mustard.

3. Using wet hands, divide the sausage meat into 6 egg-size balls. Spread the bread crumbs in a dish.

4. Take a ball of sausage meat and spread it out into a disk in the palm of your hand. Lay an egg on it and gently work the sausage meat until it smoothly encases the egg. Drop it into the bread crumbs and roll it around until covered.

5. Heat the oil in a pan and gently cook the Scotch eggs until golden brown all over.

RECIPE TESTED BY KATE

TIPS

o Try making variations by mixing some blood sausage or chorizo into the meat.

o If you want to show off, boil the eggs so that the yolks are still slightly soft.

o Use duck's or quail's eggs to make Scotch eggs in alternative sizes. A hot Scotch duck egg with a little green salad makes the classiest appetizer you could imagine.

o Some books will tell you to deep-fry them—no, no, we disagree.

ROASTED CANNED ARTICHOKES

Preparation time: 1 minute
Cooking time: 10 minutes
♥ ✓ WF DF GF V

1 can or jar of **artichoke hearts in oil**
extra **olive oil**, if necessary

1. Preheat the oven to 400°F.

2. Arrange the artichokes in a baking pan or in an ovenproof dish. If they have not been previously kept in oil, brush them liberally with olive oil.

3. Put into the oven for 10 minutes.

4. Store on a plate in the refrigerator for when hunger strikes.

TIPS

o You can grill the artichokes on the stove in a ridged grill pan, if you prefer.

RECIPE TESTED BY PETA

PRESERVED FLAVORS

People have always needed to preserve their food, especially in countries where winter can spell famine. The autumnal bumper crops of fruit and vegetables had to be made to last until spring. Any surplus livestock—too costly to keep alive over winter—would be butchered and then salted, smoked, or potted. Great ribbons of sausages would hang from the rafters. Strong fingers would tie hams to pegs driven into soft chimney brick.

Preservation techniques take their cue from the climate. In the damp forests of northern Europe, unsuitable for sun- or wind-drying, people there have relied largely on fermenting, pickling, smoking, salting, and (more recently, after sugar started arriving from the West Indies) sugaring. These techniques have helped define national palates. The British love pickles and cheeses. The Portuguese write ballads to their bacalhau (salt cod). The Germans pile their fermented cabbage (sauerkraut) high with salted sausages. In Sweden, surströmming—fermented fish—was developed at a time when salting was too expensive.

These days—when we can buy anything we want, whenever we want—we tend to view preserving as a form of experimental cooking, for those with time on their hands. But it can be much more than that. Not only does it create bold, flavorful morsels that can be eaten when you have less time on your hands—it is also a great way to get in touch with your culinary roots.

These recipes have been developed for the British market, where preserving foods by canning in a boiling-water canner or pressure canner is not considered necessary. For our American readers, where preservng guidelines are different, our advice is that you store these preserves for no longer than the recommended times given in the recipes. Alternatively, visit the Web site for the National Center for Home Food Preparation, which provides canning advice based on the United States Department of Agriculture (USADA) guidelines.

PICKLING

Time was when the onset of fall—with a bumper crop and the promise of winter famine to come—would be greeted by a frenzy of pickling. Preserving vegetables in vinegar (instead of salt) made sense in northern countries, where beer (and its close relation, malt vinegar) was cheap and abundant.

Vinegar also has the advantage that you don't need to soak the salt out of the vegetables before eating them. And they retain a satisfyingly fresh crunch. If necessity is the mother of invention, the pickle is one of her most talented offspring.

PICKLING by Katie

This year has been a revelation. We've moved to the country. We have a vegetable garden, in which things grow. Some of them I recognize, and have even planted, but others have been a wonderful, confusing, and somehow successful mystery. Call it work ethic, call it guilt, but I can't bear the idea of waste. Especially if Mother Nature's been good enough to provide me with loads of sometimes ugly but free and tasty fruit and vegetables. And so my voyage into the world of pickles, chutneys, jellies, and jams has begun. I've had to read a lot of books, and talk to many of my friends' aunts. I've bought a really huge stainless steel stockpot—stainless steel is best for acidic ingredients, such as vinegar—and a jelly bag. I've discovered the wonders of Web sites. And after considerable trial and error, and some really nasty episodes with burned sugar (and burned tongues), I've had the satisfaction of sticking labels on jars and filling up a shelf in the pantry with stuff I've made. From our garden.

Katie's top tips for making chutney

○ The ratio of fruit/vegetables : vinegar : sugar will vary depending on the sweetness and acidity of the fruit and vegetables, but as a rule you can start with about 6½ lb : 4 cups : 2½ cups and adjust for taste. Don't be frightened and feel tied to recipes; the beauty of chutney is that you can use almost any fruit or vegetable, and experiments with spices work.

○ Don't shred your fruit and veg too fine, because you'll end up with a spicy puree, but don't be TOO haphazard with your chopping. Just think about having half an onion falling out of your sandwich. Make those pieces bite-size.

○ Readers in the United States should visit the National Center for Home Food Preparation's web site if they would like to can these preserves for long-term storage.

Above (blue plate): Jossy's Onion, Orange & Sweet Pepper Chutney; Middle left: Katie's Onion Marmalade;
Middle right: Claudia's Eggplant Pickle; Below: Katie's "Chuck-it-all-in Chutney"

KATIE'S "CHUCK-IT-ALL-IN CHUTNEY"

Makes: 6–8 jars, depending on size
Preparation time: 30 minutes
Cooking time: 3–4 hours

♥ DF V

My father-in-law, Leon (yes, that one), went into the greenhouse at the end of September and picked all the green tomatoes. "There you are," he said. "Now you can make chutney." *Katie*

4½ lb **green tomatoes** or ripe **red tomatoes**
4 **onions**
3 **apples**
6 **plums**
2 fresh **green chiles**
1¾ cups **raisins** or **dried currants**, or a mixture
1 level tablespoon **salt**
2 cups **firmly packed brown sugar**
6 cloves of **garlic**
a 2 inch piece of **fresh ginger**
2 **cinnamon sticks**
10 **cloves**
5 cups **malt vinegar**, or any other vinegar

1. Chop the tomatoes and onions finely. Core the apples and pit the plums, then chop finely (you can leave the skins on the apples). Seed and chop the chiles.

2. Put all the chopped fruit, vegetables, and chiles into a big saucepan, along with the raisins or currants, salt, and sugar. Crush the garlic and add to the pan. Stir well.

3. Wrap the ginger and spices in a cheesecloth square, or an old dish towel, and tie with string, leaving the ends long enough to tie to the pan handle so that the bundle can be removed easily. Add your spice bundle to the pan with the vinegar.

4. Bring to a boil, then reduce the heat and let the chutney simmer very gently for about 3 hours. Stir occasionally. You'll know the consistency is about right when you can drag a spoon through the mixture and it leaves a trail that doesn't immediately fill up with vinegar.

5. Pour the hot chutney into sterilized jars (you can't skimp on the sterilizing part, see right) and seal the lids and screw bands.

6. Label when it's cold, refrigerate, and DON'T EAT IT for AT LEAST a week. The flavors mellow, and it's much more delicious. It will keep for up to a month in the refrigerator.

How to sterilize jars for chutneys and jams:

Put clean, washed Mason-style canning jars—the type with a lid and separate screw band—along with the lids in a large pot on top of a rack or dish towel and add enough water to have 1 inch above the jars. Bring to a boil and boil for 10 minutes plus 1 minute for every 1,000 feet above sea level. Reduce the heat to simmering and keep in the water until needed.

FRIENDS & FAMILY RECIPES

CLAUDIA'S EGGPLANT PICKLE (*Brinjal Kasaundi*)

A sensational pickle to serve with curries, with leftover rice or cold meat.

Makes: 1 large jar
Preparation time: 10 minutes
Cooking time: 40 minutes
♥ WF DF GF V

2 **eggplants** (about 2¼ lb)
1 **fresh red chile**, seeded
a 2 inch piece of **fresh ginger**
8 cloves of **garlic**
1 tablespoon **ground cumin**
1 cup **wine vinegar**
1 cup **toasted sesame oil**
1 tablespoon **mustard seeds**
1 teaspoon **fenugreek seeds**
6 **curry leaves**
1 teaspoon **turmeric**
½ cup **sugar**
sea salt

1. First, sterilize your jars (see page 254).

2. Cut the eggplants into ¾ inch slices. Blend the chile, ginger, garlic, and cumin with a little of the vinegar in a food processor.

3. Heat 3 tablespoons of the oil in a large saucepan and add the mustard and fenugreek seeds. When they start to crackle, add the curry leaves along with the ginger and chili paste. Cook until the mixture begins to brown.

4. Add the turmeric, sugar, and remaining vinegar and stir well. Add the eggplants, season with salt, and bring to a boil. Simmer gently for about 30 minutes.

5. Let the mixture to cool, then pour it into a jar. Cover with the remaining oil. This will keep for one month in the refrigerator.

TIPS

o Depending on the size of your jar, you may need to add a little more oil to cover the eggplants.

Claudia Roden has been a friend of my mother since I was a child. She has an encyclopedic knowledge of Middle Eastern and Mediterranean food, which she passes on with a gentle and warm enthusiasm. She is also a spectacular cook. We have a test at Leon when we are devising dishes for the menu: would we be proud to serve it to Claudia? This recipe is one she found in the Bene Israel Jewish community in India, and first appeared in *The Book of Jewish Food*. If you have never used any of her cookbooks, you have a treat in store.
Henry

FRIENDS & FAMILY RECIPES

Claudia Roden

JOSSY'S ONION, ORANGE & SWEET PEPPER CHUTNEY

Makes: 3 large jars
Preparation time: 40 minutes
Cooking time: 1 hour 15 minutes

♥ WF DF GF V

2 fresh **red chiles**
6 cloves of **garlic**
a 2 inch piece of **fresh ginger**
3 large **onions**
1 large **orange bell pepper**
3 large **oranges**
10 **cardamom pods**
1 teaspoon **turmeric**
2 teaspoons **black onion seeds**
1 heaping cup **granulated sugar**
1¼ lb **white wine vinegar**
sea salt

1. First, sterilize your jars (see page 254).

2. Seed and slice the chiles, and peel and finely slice the garlic and ginger.

3. Peel the onions and cut into quarters, then slice finely. Seed the bell pepper and cut into fairly small pieces.

4. Squeeze the orange juice into a heavy saucepan. Scrape the pith out of the orange halves and discard, then cut the skins into small pieces and add to the pan with the chiles and garlic.

5. Lightly crush the cardamom pods and add to the pan with the turmeric, onion seeds, sugar, vinegar, and 1¼ cups of water. Season with salt, stir well, and bring the mixture to a boil. Simmer as gently as you can, uncovered, for about 1 hour, stirring occasionally.

6. Pour into the jars, seal with the lids and screw bands when cooled, and store in the refrigerator. It will keep for 3 weeks.

KATIE'S ONION MARMALADE

This is a bit classier than the Chuck-It-All-In Chutney, and doesn't take as long to make. But you have to keep it in the refrigerator. It's inspired by Sarah Raven's fantastic *Garden Cookbook*.

Makes: 2 small jars
Preparation time: 10 minutes
Cooking time: 40 minutes
♥ WF DF GF V

4 **onions**
2 cloves of **garlic**
olive oil
¼ cup **red wine**
¼ cup **balsamic vinegar**
1 tablespoon **packed brown sugar**
1 sprig of **fresh thyme**
sea salt and **freshly ground black pepper**

1. First, sterilize your jars (see page 254).

2. Slice the onions finely, and crush the garlic.

3. Heat the olive oil in a heavy saucepan, and gently cook the onion and garlic for 20 minutes, being careful not to let them brown.

4. Add the wine, vinegar, and sugar, and simmer very slowly until most of the liquid has evaporated.

5. Add the thyme, salt, and pepper, and cook for a few additional minutes. You can leave the thyme in if you've stripped the leaves and chopped them. If you just dropped the stems in whole, for flavor, take them out.

6. Pour into hot sterilized jars and seal with the lids and screw bands when cooled. This will keep in the refrigerator for up to 3 weeks.

FRIENDS & FAMILY
RECIPES

JOJO'S LEMON & UGLY LIME MARMALADE

Jojo Tulloh is our gardening guru and author of the wonderful *Freshly Picked*. She often gives this as a Christmas present to people who love homemade marmalade. They will usually have run out by then and be suffering marmalade withdrawal while waiting for the new season's Sevilles to arrive in mid-January.

Jojo in her garden, summer 2009

Makes: 5 large jars
Preparation time: 30 minutes
Cooking time: 2 hours
♥ WF DF GF V

6 **lemons**
2 round **Indian green limes**
2 yellow **grapefruits**
1 **ugly lime**, or kaffir limes as they are commonly known
12½ cups **unbleached granulated sugar**

1. Scrub the lemons and green limes and cut them in half. Squeeze the juice into a bowl and keep the seeds. Set the bowl of juice aside. Cut the skins into thin julienne strips and place in a large, stainless steel stockpot.

2. Peel the skin from the grapefruit and the ugly lime with a vegetable peeler. Cut the pith from the grapefruit flesh, remove and keep any seeds, and put the flesh into the pan. Put the peeled ugly lime, all the seeds, and the pith into a cheesecloth jelly bag and tie up with string.

3. Chop the grapefruit and ugly lime skins into thin strips and add to the pan with 13¼ cups of water and the jelly bag. Simmer gently for 1½ hours. When the peel is soft, take the jelly bag out and squeeze it to get all the juice out into the pan (this will help the marmalade set).

4. Put a couple of saucers into the freezer. Measure the mixture in the pan and add 2¼ cups of sugar for every 2 cups of mixture. Then add the reserved lemon and lime juice and put the pan on low heat.

5. Bring to a simmer until the sugar has dissolved, then boil rapidly. After 15 minutes, start testing to see if your marmalade is ready—it shouldn't take longer than 45 minutes. (Test this by taking a saucer out of the freezer. Put a teaspoon of marmalade on the saucer, wait a minute, then push the mixture with your finger. If it wrinkles, your marmalade has reached setting point.)

6. Let the marmalade cool for 30 minutes, stirring occasionally, then pour into your sterilized jars (see page 254 for tips on sterilizing your jars). Let cool, seal, and refrigerate for up to 3 weeks.

Ramekin above: Blackberry Compote
Middle: Strawberry Compote
Below: Jojo's Lemon & Ugly Lime Marmalade

FRIENDS & FAMILY RECIPES

JOSSY'S FRESH APRICOT & CITRUS JAM *with pine nuts*

This heavenly jam is wonderful stirred into plain yogurt—or spread on toast or croissants for breakfast, of course. As with everything, this is best made in season.

Makes: 6 jars
Preparation time: 10 minutes
Cooking time: about 30 minutes
♥ WF GF DF V

4 lb large **fresh apricots**
1¼ cups **fresh orange juice**
⅛ cup **lemon juice**
8¾ cups **granulated sugar**
1 (3 oz) pouch of **liquid pectin**
⅛ cup **pine nuts**
15g **unsalted butter**
3–4 teaspoons **apricot brandy**—optional

1. First, sterilize your jars (see page 254).

2. Meanwhile, halve the apricots and put them into a large, stainless steel stockpot, discarding the pits. Pour the orange juice into a liquid measuring cup, add the lemon juice, and bring the total amount of liquid up to 2 cups with water.

3. Add the liquid to the apricots. Put the pan over high heat, bring to a boil, then lower the heat and simmer gently for 10–15 minutes, or until the apricots are soft but not mushy.

4. Remove the pan from the heat and add the sugar, stirring until it dissolves.

5. Heat a dry skillet and toss the pine nuts around for a minute or two to brown. Add them to the pan with the butter. Return the pan to high heat, bring the jam to a roiling boil that cannot be stirred down. Add the pecin and boil, stirring continuously, for 1 minute, or follow the package directions.

6. Add the apricot brandy, if using, and leave the jam to settle for 15 minutes. Ladle the jam into the sterilized jars, then when cooled, seal with the lids and screw bands. Refrigerate for up to 3 weeks.

STRAWBERRY COMPOTE

Makes: 1⅛ cups, feeds: 4
Preparation time: 2 minutes
Cooking time: 20 minutes
♥ ✓ WF GF DF V

1 pint **strawberries**, frozen or fresh
juice of ½ a **lemon**
1 tablespoon + 1 teaspoon **fructose**

1. Combine all the ingredients in a small, heavy saucepan with a lid.

2. Bring the ingredients to a gentle boil and let bubble for 5 minutes, then remove the lid.

3. Simmer for another 15 minutes, or until the fruit collapses and the sauce is thickish—it thickens as it cools. Pour into jars and serve, or store in the refrigerator.

PETRA'S QUINCE JELLY

Perfect on toast, with cheese, with cold leftover meat, with everything.

Makes: 6 medium jars
Preparation time: 10 minutes
Cook time: 2 hours
♥ WF GF DF V

3¾ lb **quinces**
3 **apples**
granulated sugar
2 **lemons**

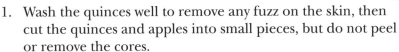

Petra and Jeremy in the Hebrides, June 1967

RECIPE TESTED BY. JEREMY

1. Wash the quinces well to remove any fuzz on the skin, then cut the quinces and apples into small pieces, but do not peel or remove the cores.

2. Place in a stainless steel pan and cover with water. Put a lid on the pan and simmer gently until tender; this may take up to 2 hours.

3. Pour the contents of the pan into a jelly bag and let stand for 12 hours, suspended over a bowl. To each 2½ cups of juice, add 2¼ cups of sugar and the juice of ½ a lemon.

4. Bring the liquid to a boil, then let boil gently until it sets; it should take about 20 minutes (see page 259 for tips on setting).

5. Pour into sterilized jars (see page 254), let cool, and seal with lids and screw bands. It will keep for up to 3 weeks in the refrigerator.

My mother and father-in-law dedicate months (or so it seems) every year to dealing with the glut of quinces that grow in their London garden. They have cooked every possible recipe that involves quinces, but this jelly is always the number one. Family members beg to have their quotas increased. *Henry*

BLACKBERRY COMPOTE & SPICES

An autumnal compote with a warm spiciness. A staple on the Leon menu.

Feeds: 4
Preparation time: 2 minutes
Cooking time: 20 minutes
♥ ✓ WF DF GF V

2 cups **blackberries**, frozen or fresh
juice of ¼ of a **lemon**
2 tablespoons **fructose**
a pinch of **ground cinnamon**
a pinch of **ground star anise**

RECIPE TESTED BY. EMMA

1. Simply combine all the ingredients in a small, heavy saucepan and cover with a lid.

2. Bring to a gentle boil, and after 5 minutes remove the lid.

3. Simmer for another 15 minutes, until the fruit has collapsed and the sauce is thickish—it will thicken as it cools. Serve or store in the refrigerator.

TIPS

○ Great in plain yogurt, on toast, on ice cream, on oatmeal. We could go on.

○ Will keep in the refrigerator for a few days.

POTTING

The precursor of canning and vacuum-packing, "potting" is one of the simplest ways to preserve food. It works by killing off any bacteria contained within the food and then shutting out the germs.

Its major advantage from a gastronomic perspective is that the barrier used to shut out the germs tends to be a flavor-rich layer of fat. Yum.

As a quick lunch, it is hard to better some hot toast topped with a little terrine or potted meat, which is similar to a pâte, from this section and a smear of pickle from the last. Heaven.

POTTED MEATS

A great way to use up leftover roasts of any kind—spread on sourdough toast and served with a little chutney.

Feeds: 2–4
Preparation time: 10 minutes
Cooking time: 5 minutes
+ 1 hour to set
✓ WF GF

1 stick **unsalted butter**
1 **bay leaf**
1 cup finely chopped, cold **cooked meat**
½ teaspoon **cayenne**
zest of 1 **lemon**
a good scratch of **nutmeg**
sea salt and **freshly ground black pepper**

1. Put the butter and the bay leaf into a small saucepan and place over gentle heat until the butter has melted.

2. Put the chopped, cold meat into a bowl and stir in the butter (as you pour the butter in, you can leave the watery deposit at the bottom of the pan, effectively clarifying it). Remove and reserve the bay leaf.

3. Add the lemon zest, nutmeg, and cayenne and season well with salt and pepper.

4. Mix well, then put into a small dish or jar, squashing the meat down so that it is all coated in butter. Put the bay leaf on top and put in the refrigerator for an hour or so to set. It will keep for a month in the refrigerator.

JOHN BUCHAN'S TERRINE

A simple terrine, perfect with some strong chutney.

Feeds: 8–10
Preparation time: 30 minutes
Cooking time: 1½ hours
✓ WF GF

12 slices of **smoked bacon**
1 small **onion**
1 lb **pork belly**
10 oz **pork loin cutlets**
1 teaspoon **ground coriander**
2 **eggs**
3 tablespoons **heavy cream**
1 cup white wine
sea salt and **cracked black pepper**

1. Preheat the oven to 350°F.

2. Line a 10 inch long terrine dish with the bacon, leaving any excess hanging over the edge. Finely chop the onion.

3. Carefully remove the skin from the pork belly (you can oil and salt it, then roast it in a high oven for 90 minutes to make scratchings). Cube the belly flesh and the pork loin and put them into a food processor with the onion, coriander, eggs, and cream. Pour in the white wine and 3 healthy pinches of sea salt and some pepper. Now blend everything together until you have little pea-size pieces of meat.

4. Put the mixture into the terrine and flip the excess bacon slices over the top. Put the terrine into a deep oven pan and pour water into the pan so that it comes halfway up the sides of the terrine.

5. Cook in the oven for 1½ hours, uncovered, then remove and let cool at room temperature before serving.

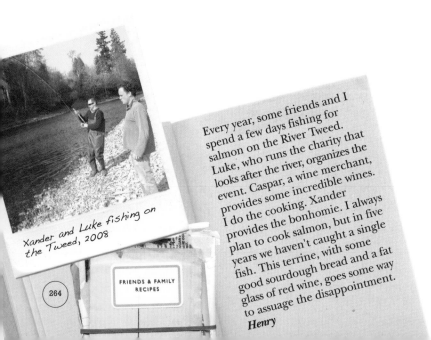

Xander and Luke fishing on the Tweed, 2008

FRIENDS & FAMILY RECIPES

Every year, some friends and I spend a few days fishing for salmon on the River Tweed. Luke, who runs the charity that looks after the river, organizes the event. Caspar, a wine merchant, provides some incredible wines. I do the cooking. Xander provides the bonhomie. I always plan to cook salmon, but in five years we haven't caught a single fish. This terrine, with some good sourdough bread and a fat glass of red wine, goes some way to assuage the disappointment.

Henry

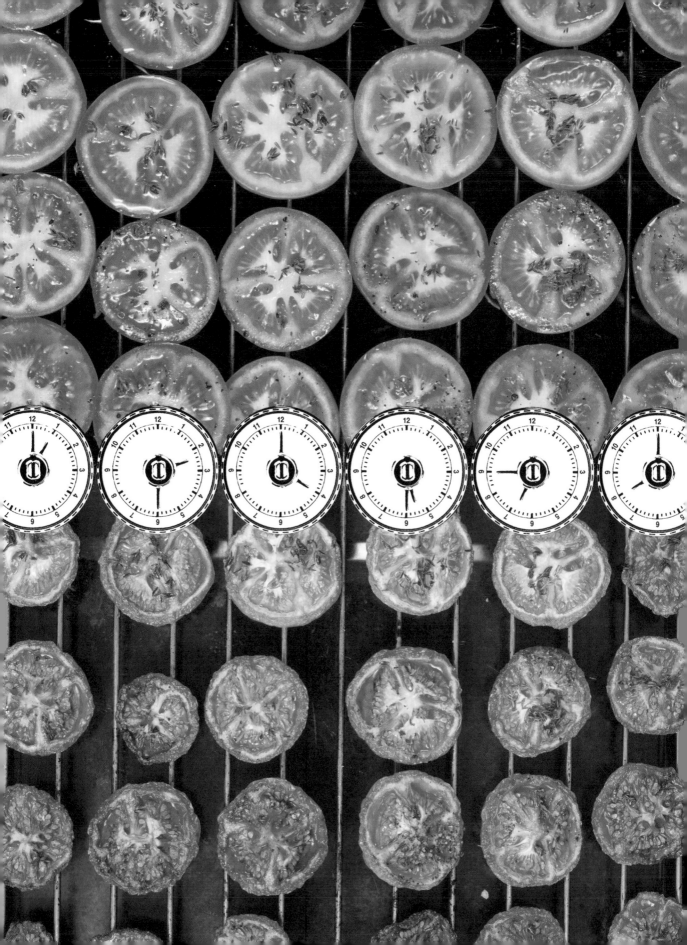

"SUN-DRIED" TOMATOES

These "sun-dried" tomatoes taste far fresher than store-bought ones, and are really simple to make. Once you have got the hang of making them, you will never go back.

Makes: 1 medium jar
Preparation time: 5 minutes
Cooking time: 7 hours
♥ ✓ WF DF GF V

4 medium **tomatoes**
2 teaspoons **sea salt**
1 teaspoon **freshly ground black pepper**
a sprig of **fresh thyme**
olive oil
1 clove of **garlic**

1. Preheat the oven to 120–140°F, or if you have a gas oven, as low as you can set it. (Beware! If it is higher than 140°F, the tomatoes will cook instead of dry).

2. Cut the tomatoes in half, place in a baking sheet, and sprinkle with salt, pepper, thyme, and 1 tablespoon of olive oil.

3. Put into the oven and let dry for about 7 hours, or overnight.

4. Transfer to a sterilized jar (see page 254) and cover with olive oil, the sliced garlic, and the thyme before sealing with the lid.

5. These will keep in the refrigerator for 3 weeks.

TIPS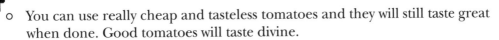

o You can use really cheap and tasteless tomatoes and they will still taste great when done. Good tomatoes will taste divine.

o The trick to these is to get the balance of time and heat right. If your oven is too low, they will retain too much moisture in them and will not keep well (although they will taste plump and fine). If the oven is too hot, they will be partly cooked—again delicious, but not what we are after. You might need to experiment with a couple of batches before you work out what is best for your oven.

o A convection setting in the oven works best, because it takes out the moisture much more effectively.

Opposite: "Sun-dried" Tomatoes before and after drying

LEON STRATEGY SALAMI

It takes some time and preparation, but there is something life-changing about biting into a slice of homemade salami. This recipe is only for guidance—please seek additional advice about the fermenting and curing process from a sausage-making book.

Makes: 6–8 salamis
Preparation time: A lot
(leave a lazy afternoon)
Curing time: 4 weeks–3 months
✓ WF DF GF

Equipment needed:
– a grinder with sausage
stuffer attachment
– butcher's string
meat thermometer

2 long **natural hog casings**, soaked overnight in cold water
2 teaspoons **fennel seeds**
1 clove of **garlic**
4 lb **pork shoulder butt**
1 lb **pork fat** (ask your butcher for back fat)
2 teaspoons **black peppercorns**
2 tablespoons **dextrose**
1 teaspoon **Cure #2**
about 3 tablespoons **kosher salt**—2 percent of the weight of the meat + fat
1¾ cups **red wine**
starter culture—see package instructions for recommended amount

1. Put each end of a casing up to the faucet and rinse through with cold water. Put into a fresh bowl of cold water.

2. Dry roast the fennel in a pan. Peel the garlic and crush finely. Coarsely grind the pork shoulder. Chop the pork fat into little squares (like the ones you get in a salami).

3. Put all the ingredients except for the wine and starter culture into a bowl and mix thoroughly (keeping the peppercorns whole). Make sure you measure your salt carefully. Too much and it will be too salty, too little and the salami may turn rotten. Check the meat temperature; if it is not 40°F, refrigerate until it is.

4. Add the wine and starter culture to a bowl, add the chilled meat, and mix until the meat has absorbed the wine.

5. Now, fill your sausage stuffer. Stick two fingers into the end of a casing and dip it under the water, then slide the whole casing onto the end of your sausage stuffer.

6. Squeeze out a little of the mixture to make sure there is no air in the casing. Fold over the casing and tie it with a single knot, then flip over the loose end and tie it again. Fill the casing carefully, making it as tight and air-free as possible without tearing the casing.

7. When you have a sausage at 8–10 inches long, tie it off again with a single knot, then flip it over and tie a double knot. Leave enough loose string to hang the salami. Continue until you are out of mixture.

8. Follow the recommendations on the starter culture package to fement the sausages at the correct temperature and humidity and for the recommended amount of time.

9. Now, transfer the salamis to a refrigerator at 45–55°F with a relative humidity of 75 percent to dry for about 70–80 days.

Every year we take a few days away from Leon, to think about our strategy for the coming months. When the work is done we have some kind of feast, which usually involves butchering one of my step-mother's pigs and turning it into all manner of products—including this salami. *Henry*

SMOKING

There is a man who lives near Henry in Hackney who smokes his own salmon in his yard. It is sublime. But it took him about 30 trial salmon to get it that way. The first drafts were salty and inedible. Unless you are willing to invest the time and the cash, smoking is one of those preserving techniques best left to the professionals. However, the organic-farmed bought stuff is sustainable, cheap, and can be very good. There is a lot that you can do with it.

Our 6 favorite quick things to do with smoked salmon

1 **Put it on tagliatelle.** Heat some peas in heavy cream. Pepper it well (you shouldn't need salt). Drop in chunks of smoked salmon just before putting it on the pasta. Squeeze a some fresh lemon juice on top.

2 **Make a salad.** Peel and seed a cucumber, then chop it. Mix it with some cooked fava beans (press them out of their grayish jackets if you have the patience). Add some chopped mint, lemon juice, olive oil, and chunks of smoked salmon. Season.

3 **Drop it onto scrambled egg or into an omelet.** It's just very good.

4 **Make fake gravadlax:** Process the following ingredients and drizzle them on top: 1 tablespoon of Dijon mustard, ⅓ cup of heavy cream, 1 tablespoon of honey, a large handful of dill, and 1 tablespoon of white wine vinegar, and season with salt and pepper.

5 **Serve it as an appetizer with beets and horseradish:** Boil a couple of whole beets until soft, and peel them when cool (or buy them prepared, whole). Chop the beets into ½ inch cubes, chuck them into a bowl, and drizzle with a tablespoon of balsamic vinegar and a teaspoon of olive oil. Season with salt and pepper and sprinkle with some chopped parsley. Lay the smoked salmon on a plate and spead the beets and store-bought creamed horseradish over it.

6 **Use it to create a quick Ceviche.** If you can't get hold of good raw fish, you can make the ceviche recipe on page 148 with smoked salmon, only do not use the olive oil and be very liberal with the lemon juice to counteract the richness of the salmon.

FREEZING

Until recently, freezing was only a preservation option for the rich and for glacier dwellers. First trialed in Mesopotamia 4,000 years ago, ice houses were perfected by the Victorians to store their precious ice creams.

There are many things that can be made in advance and frozen—we normally have an assortment of stocks, soups, and stews in our freezers (see page 12). The ultimate freezer treat, however, has to be ice cream. Making homemade ice cream is much simpler than most people think.

You will need some kind of ice cream machine to proceed beyond this point.

> If you do not have an ice cream maker, all you need is a good timer and a mixer.
> 1. After you have made your ice cream mixture, transfer it into a plastic container or bowl, preferably with a lid.
> 2. Place it in the freezer for a couple of hours, or until it starts to solidify around the edges.
> 3. Remove it from the freezer and beat it thoroughly with a handheld whisk or electric mixer.
> 4. Return it to the freezer for another two hours, and then repeat the beating process. Do this a few more times until the ice cream is set.
> 5. Don't forget to remove it from the freezer well in advance so that you can scoop it out easily.

VANILLA ICE CREAM

This is the base for almost all ice creams. Once you have mastered it, you can experiment by adding fruit, rum and raisins, salted caramel, you name it …

Makes: 3¾ cups
Preparation time: 20 minutes
+ freezing time
WF GF

5 **egg yolks**
1 **vanilla bean**
2 cups **heavy cream**
½ cup **milk**
1 cup **superfine sugar** or **granulated sugar**
sea salt

1. Make sure the eggs are at room temperature. You will only be using the yolks for this recipe.

2. Halve the vanilla bean lengthwise and put it into a saucepan with the cream, milk, and sugar. Bring to a boil, stirring to make sure the sugar dissolves. Let stand for 5 minutes.

3. Meanwhile, put the egg yolks into a blender and blend for 5 minutes, or until they turn creamy. Add a small pinch of salt.

4. Bring the cream back to a boil and pour it slowly onto the eggs, blending as you work. Assuming that the cream is good and hot and the eggs not too cold, you should be left with great not-too-thick custard. (If you want to make it thicker, heat it gently on the stove, but you shouldn't need to.)

5. Let it cool to room temperature, then pour it through a strainer into an ice cream machine and freeze. It will be best within 4 days (even in the freezer).

Back: Deep Chocolate Ice Cream; Front: Vanilla Ice Cream & Raspberry Ripple

DEEP CHOCOLATE ICE CREAM

We have experimented for some time to get a deep, dark chocolate ice cream. The breakthrough came when we added unsweetened cocoa powder—traditionally looked down on. It adds real depth of flavor and improves the texture.

Makes: 3¾ cups
Preparation time: 20 minutes
+ freezing time
WF GF V

RECIPE TESTED BY GLENYS

5 **egg yolks**
½ cup **milk**
2 tablespoons **heavy cream**
3 oz **chocolate** (70 percent cocoa solids)
⅔ cup **superfine sugar** or **granulated sugar**
⅛ cup **unsweetened cocoa powder**

1. Make sure the eggs are at room temperature. You will only be using the yolks for this recipe.

2. Bring the milk and cream to a boil. Add the chocolate and let it melt.

3. Put the egg yolks into a bowl, add the sugar and cocoa, and beat well. Beat in a little of the hot cream/milk mixture, then put everything into a saucepan and return it to the stove. Heat gently, stirring well, for 10 minutes. It will bubble—don't worry.

4. Pour through a strainer and let cool.

5. Freeze in an ice cream machine. Best eaten within 4 days.

TIPS

○ Make some hazelnut cracknell (see page 194) and add it to the machine when it is a little stiff but still not frozen.

RASPBERRY RIPPLE

You can omit the vodka if you are making this for children, but it really lifts the flavor of the raspberries (and the spirits).

Makes: 3¾ cups
Preparation time: 20 minutes
WF GF V

vanilla ice cream (see page 273)
1 pint of **raspberries**
¼ cup **confectioners' sugar**
2 tablespoons **vodka**

1. Make the vanilla ice cream.

2. Put the raspberries, confectioners' sugar, and vodka into a blender and process to a thickish puree.

3. Before the ice cream is fully frozen (but once it is pretty stiff), stir through the raspberries in thick seams. Continue to freeze.

SACHA'S CANJA

A last word. We couldn't find a proper space for this recipe, but we love it, so we put it here. A wonderful dish for when you are feeling lousy.

Feeds: 4
Preparation time: 10 minutes
Cooking time: 15 minutes
♥ ✓ WF GF

1 **onion**
8 oz **chicken thighs**
olive oil
1 cup **basmati** or **long-grain rice**
3¾ cups **chicken stock**
2 tablespoons **crème fraîche** or **heavy cream**
sea salt and **freshly ground black pepper**

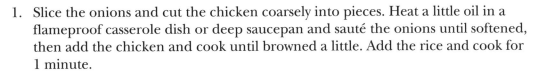

1. Slice the onions and cut the chicken coarsely into pieces. Heat a little oil in a flameproof casserole dish or deep saucepan and sauté the onions until softened, then add the chicken and cook until browned a little. Add the rice and cook for 1 minute.

2. Add the chicken stock to the dish and cook for 10 minutes, or until the rice is tender.

3. Add the crème fraîche or cream and season with salt and pepper.

TIPS

o You can use leftover chicken from a roast—just add it toward the end of the cooking time.

o Add more stock if you want it to be more of a soup.

o Serve with Parmesan shavings and a drizzle of olive oil, or with a spoonful of harissa (pictured).

o Serve with crusty bread and a green salad.

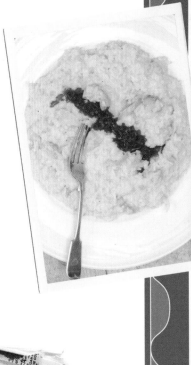

Sacha (far right) with the family, 1950

Sacha—my wife Katie's aunt—used to live in Brazil, and this is an adaptation of one of her recipes. Great for when you are feeling stressed, or just as an easy dinner.
John

FRIENDS & FAMILY RECIPES

BONUS FEATURES

Cocktails

Cocktails are bad, which is what makes them so nice. A dream in a glass; a beach welcome; a Christmas sing-song with Dean Martin. Possibilities. Maybe even probabilities.

Tom is the king of the silver shaker at Leon. Strictly speaking, his job is to oversee the restaurant managers, but old habits die hard—he was a bartender before joining Leon, and at all our parties, you'll find him back in Tom Cruise mode, juggling bottles of arcane liquors with his former colleague and conspirator, Giles. By the end of the evening, he'll be on the dance floor reaping the rewards of his making.

These are Tom's top six tipples. Proceed with care. Over to you Tom …

CHRISTMAS COCKTAIL

I first drank this in a fashionable Soho bar and realized immediately that my mom would love it. I made it last Christmas for the family. Mom did love it, Dad drank far too much of it. Substitute berry syrup for Campari and use club soda instead of prosecco, and the kids can join in, too.

Feeds: 6

½ cup **Campari**
¼ cup **lemon juice**
½ cup **clementine juice**
¼ cup **sugar syrup** (see below)
1¾ cups **prosecco**
orange zest, for garnish

Sugar syrup: Put equal parts superfine sugar and tap water (1 cup and 1 cup) into a small pitcher, stir, and let stand (stirring occasionally) until the sugar dissolves. Should take about 20 minutes.

1. In a cocktail shaker, combine the Campari, lemon juice, clementine juice, and sugar syrup.

2. Add ice and shake.

3. Strain the mixture equally into 6 champagne glasses and top with prosecco. Garnish with a twist of orange zest.

HOT HALLOWEEN PUNCH

It was Halloween 2009, and Giles and I were at a party at the "Lady Castle" in London (a big house full of beautiful, single girls). Giles had the idea of making a hot punch—it was freezing outside. We used various bits and bobs that he found in the kitchen and came up with this. The party went with a swing, and this concoction is now a must every Halloween.

Feeds: about 20

1¾ cups **brandy**
6½ cups **hard dry cide**r
⅔ cup **sugar**
1¼ cups **lemon juice**
10 dashes of **Angostura bitters**
2–3 **cinnamon sticks**
5–6 **cloves**
lemon zest for garnish

1. Pour all the ingredients except the lemon zest into a large saucepan and bring to a slow simmer.

2. Ladle into heatproof glasses and garnish with a twist of lemon zest.

SOUL FRUIT CUP

Giles now runs his own company called Soul Shakers, traveling the world making cocktails at some of the best parties in the world (lucky boy). He put together a cocktail bar for the Regatta (a British boating event) and served his version of Pimm's. Perfect to sip on a hot summer's day, while others work up a sweat.

Feeds: 6

½ cup **gin**
⅛ cup **Campari**
½ cup **sweet vermouth**
⅔ cup **pink grapefruit juice**
juice of 2 **lemons**
6–8 slices of **cucumber**
lemonade (homemade or bottled)
strawberries and **mint** for
    garnish—optional

1. Pour the alcohol, grapefruit juice, and lemon juice into a pitcher.

2. Add the cucumber and lemonade and stir.

3. Pour into iced glasses and garnish with strawberries and/or mint, if you desire.

LEON SUMMER PUNCH

Think summer, all your best friends, your backyard, a balmy evening and a victory in your favourite ball game.

Feeds: 6

16 **strawberries**
2 **pears** (nice and ripe)
⅜ cup **sugar syrup** (see page 278)
⅜ cup **vodka**
½ cup **lemon juice**
bottle of prosecco

1. Blend the strawberries and pears to make a simple puree, adding the sugar syrup to sweeten.

2. Put the puree into a pitcher and mix in the vodka and lemon juice.

3. Top with prosecco and stir. Pour into champagne flutes and toast the sports hero of the day.

VODKA ESPRESSO

This drink has been a favorite of the London bar scene since the mid-nineties. Rumor has it that its birthplace was the Pharmacy—the artist Damien Hirst's now defunct joint in Notting Hill. An experienced barman can tell how many of these caffeine-loaded cocktails a customer has had from the twitching in the arm or the judder of the head. Be warned: After three, it is almost impossible to sit down.

Feeds: 1

2½ tablespoons **vodka**
1 tablespoon **Kahlua**
2 tablespoons **espresso**
superfine sugar
coffee beans for garnish
   —optional

1. In a cocktail shaker, combine the vodka, Kahlua, espresso, and a dash of sugar (it's up to you how sweet you like it). Pack it full of ice and shake it really hard for about 10 seconds—you want a nice froth on top, so shake it good.

2. Pour into a martini glass or champagne flute and garnish with 3 coffee beans, if you have them.

3. This recipe is for one cocktail. You can probably fit two in one shaker, but any more than that and you'll lose the lovely crème on top.

KAMOMILLA FIZZ

This is a slightly more taxing drink, for those of you who see yourselves as cocktail connoisseurs. I invented it for the International Finlandia Vodka Cup in 2006. It won the best long drink and we served bucketloads at the Big Chill the same year. The camomile and cucumber work wonderfully together, and it's a great long summer drink. You can substitute the vodka with gin, which also works really well (it's known as a 10cc).

Feeds: 1

3 slices of **cucumber** (about ⅛ inch thick)
½ a **lemon**, cut into 4 wedges
5 teaspoons **camomile tea syrup** (see below)
2½ tablespoons **vodka**
ice
sparkling water or **club soda**

In a cocktail shaker, muddle the cucumber and 3 of the lemon wedges with the camomile tea syrup. Muddle it hard to work the juice and oil out of the lemon. Add the vodka and ice and shake for a good 10 seconds. Strain into an ice-filled highball glass. Top with sparkling water or club soda. Garnish with the remaining lemon wedge. Kippis!

Camomile tea syrup: Make a strong brew of camomile tea—about 3 teabags in 1 cup of hot water. Let stand for 5 minutes. Remove the teabags and add 1 cup of superfine sugar, then stir until the sugar has dissolved and let cool.

Giles in Key West, 1982

FRIENDS & FAMILY RECIPES

Tom and his brother Patrick doing AC/DC, Sheffield, 1988

BEHIND THE SCENES at a Leon party ...

FROM FARMS WE TRUST

Since Leon opened in July 2004, we have relied heavily on the wisdom and experience of the people who rear our meat. Farming in the UK is hard work for little reward, and three people in particular have gone out of their way to support us as we've grown.

Andy Maunder

Andy Maunder's hands were black from picking walnuts when we first met him. We liked him immediately. Since that day, he has been in charge of making our chickens happy at his farm in Devon.

Dealing with Leon is wonderful; proper people buying proper chicken. When buying chicken, they want a great tasting product but, just as important, they want a sustainable, welfare-friendly, rural-job-creating, wildlife-promoting, natural, as it used to taste, chicken. "Proper job" as we say in the West Country. *Andy*

Basil and Richard

Basil and Richard, a father and son team also from Devon, make terrific sausages and the best additive-free bacon we have ever tasted.

Andy, Basil, and Richard. Thank you.

Leon is an exciting venture for us here at Devon Rose. We make Leon bacon and sausages from free range pork raised here on the unique Jurassic pasture land on the South Devon coast, mixed with our own blend of herbs and spices. We feel that we share their philosophy and love of great food. For Leon, we use a mixture of rare, traditional, and modern breeds, all noted for purity, taste and eating quality.

Basil (left) and son Richard (middle)

SUSTAINABILITY

Henry recently helped to set up the Sustainable Restaurant Association: a not-for-profit organization that helps restaurants to do business with a clean conscience. There are all kinds of things that restaurateurs can do to tread more lightly on the earth, from watching our water usage to using fish from sustainable stocks. You can do the same at home by following a few simple principles.

Eat much less meat and dairy

Rearing animals to turn into meat or produce milk consumes profligate quantities of water, land, and energy. If we all ate a completely vegetarian diet for two days a week, the CO_2 saved would be equivalent to building ten nuclear power stations. Switching to a more vegetable-based diet, with meat, fish, and dairy as an occasional side dish instead of the main event, has the added advantage of saving you money and making you feel—and look—a million dollars.

Eat sustainable fish

We are constantly being told to eat more fish, yet global fish stocks are in serious peril. Working out which of our scaly friends you can safely eat can seem impossibly complicated, but www.fishonline.org is a great resource.

Eat more seasonally

This becomes easier to do if you order your vegetables in a weekly seasonal delivery service or you have a good local fruit and vegetable retailer. (Otherwise it requires a keen eye and disciplined hand at the supermarket.)

Shop much more at markets and local stores

This was difficult ten years ago, but since then there has been a miraculous explosion in food markets. The sellers are more likely to know the provenance of their food (and, at farmers' markets, to have produced it themselves). As an added bonus, the food tends to be less shrouded in unnecessary packaging.

Compost your trimmings

If your yard isn't big enough for a compost pile, get a worm composter. Worms are arguably easier to manage, and certainly more fun (especially for terrorizing visiting children). They'll eat almost anything, apart from onions, garlic, citrus fruits, spicy food, meat, and fish, and turn it into a lovely rich juice which can then be sprinkled onto your plants as fertilizer.

RECIPES FROM LEON MANAGERS

The managers at Leon are some of the hardest-working, most generous, and enthusiastic people you are ever likely to meet.

They are also damn fine cooks, and extremely competitive, as we discovered at a cook-off in Henry's kitchen to get their recipes into this book.

These are the winners.

ESMARELDA'S MELK KOS (MILK PUDDING)

Feeds: 8
Preparation time: 5 minutes
Cooking time: 15 minutes

 V

2 tablespoons **flour**
2 tablespoons **cornstarch**
½ cup **sugar**
pinch of **salt**
3 **eggs**
1 **vanilla bean**
8¾ cups **milk**
1 stick **butter**
ground cinnamon for dusting

Esmarelda and her son James, 1998

1. In a large bowl, mix together the flour, cornstarch, sugar, salt, and eggs.

2. Cut the vanilla bean open and place in a large, heavy sacepan with the milk and butter.

3. Gently bring the milk mixture to a boil. As soon as the milk is boiling, remove from the heat, remove the vanilla bean, and add the flour and egg mixture slowly while stirring. The mixture will start thickening right away.

4. Place the pan back on low heat, and simmer for about 5 minutes, still stirring.

5. Remove from the heat, divide among bowls, and sprinkle the ground cinnamon on top. Eat while warm!

 TIPS

o You can use this wonderful milk pudding to make a tart. Simply make a basic flaky pie dough, line a tart pan, fill it with the milk pudding, and bake in the oven for 10 minutes at 350°F. Scatter the cinnamon on top.

FRIENDS & FAMILY RECIPES

THEO'S CHICKPEA CURRY

Theo is our manager Tom's girlfriend. She makes this with either canned chickpeas (cheap) or dried chickpeas (ridiculously cheap).

Feeds: 4
Preparation time: 10 minutes
Cooking time: about 1 hour
♥ ✓ WF DF GF V

1 **onion**
5 cloves of **garlic**
2 **red chiles**
a 3 inch piece of **fresh ginger**
2 tablespoons **oil**
1 teaspoon **turmeric**
½ teaspoon **ground cumin**
1½ teaspoons **ground coriander**
1 teaspoon **garam masala**
3 (15 oz) cans of **chickpeas (garbanzo beans)**
1 (14½ oz) can of **diced tomatoes**
2 handfuls of **fresh cilantro**
sea salt and **freshly ground black pepper**

1. Peel and finely chop the onion, garlic, and chiles. Peel, then grate, the ginger on the fine edge of your grater.

2. Heat the oil in a heavy saucepan and sauté the onion over medium heat, stirring often. Add the garlic, chiles, and ginger and sauté for 2 minutes.

3. Add the spices and sauté for another 5 minutes. You might find that it all balls up and sticks to the pan, in which case add a bit more oil.

4. Drain and rinse the chickpeas, then add to the pan, stirring to coat them well in the spices. Then add the canned tomatoes. The curry should be liquidy.

5. Simmer gently for 45 minutes to an hour, until the flavors come together and the spices don't taste bitter. Stir occasionally. If it dries up, add some stock (which I make with Marigold bouillon powder—the tastiest).

6. Chop the cilantro and add to the pan. Season with salt and pepper.

 TIPS

o Add spinach to the curry, if you desire. Put it in with the cilantro, salt, and pepper, and it will wilt down quickly.

o You can vary the flavors by adding cardamom seeds and fenugreek, or dry-roasted coriander and cumin seeds, crushed in a mortar and pestle.

Tom at Docklow Manor, 1985

OT'S HOT CHEESE: EGYPTIAN GIBNA

Feeds: 4
Preparation time: 5 minutes
Cooking time: 0 minutes
✓ WF GF V

8 oz **gibna beyda** or **Greek feta cheese**
2 tablespoons **tahini**
2 tablespoons **olive oil**
½ teaspoon **chili powder**
a handful of chopped **fresh mint**
freshly ground black pepper

1. Cut the gibna beyda or feta cheese into cubes and put into a large bowl.

2. Add the tahini, olive oil, chili powder, mint, and pepper, and stir thoroughly.

3. Eat it on warmed flat bread with cold meat and salad, or serve it with chopped mangoes.

 TIPS

○ Add more chili powder if you can handle the heat.

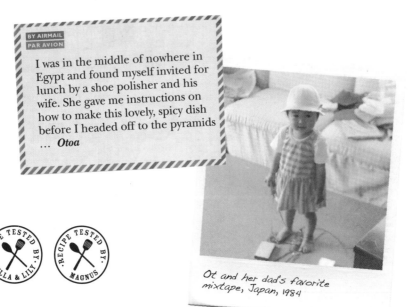

BY AIRMAIL
PAR AVION

I was in the middle of nowhere in Egypt and found myself invited for lunch by a shoe polisher and his wife. She gave me instructions on how to make this lovely, spicy dish before I headed off to the pyramids … **Otoa**

Ot and her dad's favorite mixtape, Japan, 1984

RECIPE TESTED BY: ELLA & LILY
RECIPE TESTED BY: MAGNUS

FRIENDS & FAMILY
RECIPES

ROY'S FIRE CRACKER SOUP

Feeds: 4
Preparation time: 10 minutes
Cooking time: 20 minutes
♥ ✓ WF DF GF V

3 **onions**
1 clove of **garlic**
1 **carrot**
a small piece of **fresh ginger**
1 stick of **celery**
1 tablespoon **vegetable oil**
4 cups **vegetable stock**, fresh or made with
    2 bouillon cubes
2 (14½ oz) cans of **diced tomatoes**
2 **tomatoes**
a few **fresh basil leaves**
tomato puree
½ teaspoon **mustard powder**
sea salt and **freshly ground pepper**

1. Peel and finely chop the onions and garlic. Dice the carrot, celery, and ginger.

2. Heat a small amount of oil in a saucepan and add the onions, garlic, celery, carrot, and ginger.

3. Add the stock and cook until the vegetables are soft.

4. When cooked, put everything into a blender or food processor, adding the canned and fresh tomatoes and the basil leaves. Process and return the mixture to the pan.

5. Add a generous spoonful of tomato paste, stir in the mustard powder, and season with salt and pepper.

TIPS

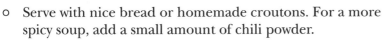

○ Serve with nice bread or homemade croutons. For a more spicy soup, add a small amount of chili powder.

○ Using too many fresh tomatoes can make the soup too sweet.

With the exception of Christmas, "bonfire" night—celebrated in the UK in November—has become the only other regular family gathering in the Bowerman household. Every year, our family comes together in my parent's backyard to watch the traditional fireworks, and we oversee this classic display with mulled wine and—in the words of my father Roy—his "fast, famous, and furious firework night soup". *Ursula*

Ursula's brother Morton, dad Roy, and mother Jennie

FRIENDS & FAMILY RECIPES

THE BIGCHILL FESTIVAL

SCREAM *IF YOU WANT TO GO* FASTER
LEON
NATURALLY FAST FOOD

THE BIG CHILL

Last summer, Leon packed its tent, unwrapped its glow sticks, and headed to Herefordshire for the Big Chill festival.

As well as manning a stall near the main stage, we cooked the cakes for a tea party in Eastnor Castle, at which Mr. Scruff served tea and Alice Russell sang.

We also served our first ever customers dressed as zombies.

PIERRE'S BIG CHILL SALAD

The highlight of the festival, at least for some of us, was a barbecue that we held backstage for Leon regulars. Henry cooked great chunks of lamb, blood sausage, butterflied chickens, and Porterhouse steaks. But the best thing was the enormous salad thrown together at the last minute by our friend Pierre.

Feeds: 4
Preparation time: 5 minutes
Cooking time: 0 minutes
♥ ✓ WF DF GF V

4 ripe **tomatoes**
a jar of **roasted bell peppers**
2 ripe **avocados**
a large handful of **fresh flat-leaf parsley**
juice of 1 **lemon**
a great glug of **olive oil**—poured from a height
a large head of **romaine lettuce**
sea salt and **freshly ground black pepper**

1. Quarter the tomatoes. Chop the bell peppers, keeping the juice from the jar. Coarsely chop the avocados and parsley. One reason this salad was so good was because of the way it was tossed. Put all the ingredients except the lettuce into a bowl and season well. Toss them energetically. Get your hands in there, up to the elbows, if necessary. The avocado should begin to break up a little. Toss it again.

2. Sit in the sun for a while. At the last moment, chop the lettuce and add to the salad. Check the seasoning again. Serve.

Pictures opposite by Rob Orchard and Steve Razzetti

DRAWERS OF WISHES

We have a chest in the Leon at Ludgate Circus with many drawers. No one knows quite how it started, but over the years it has filled up with the wishes of people who eat with us.

I wish, I wish, I wish

I wish that someone would sweep me off my feet

I wish I was a tomato

WISH I COULD GROW MY OWN VEG

I wish it wasn't too late

I WISH I COULD HEAR WHAT PEOPLE THINK

I wish I didn't have such big Books!

I WISH TO GO TO THE MOON!

I WISH everyone HAD PENS IN THEIR HAIR

I wish I wasn't full to carry on eating!

I wish I could finish my book

2009

I wish I could decide what I wanted to do with my life, which Would make me + Others happy! + I wish I had a cup of tea xx

I wish ALL THESE WISHES WOULD COME TRUE. (EXCEPT THE ONES REQUIRING SIGNIFICANT AMOUNTS OF SURGERY).

I WISH CHEESE MADE YOU THIN

I wish for my life to get easier. Selfish Arn't I? 2/9/08

I wish for a flat stomach

I wish I could fly!

I WISH I had a sausage dog called helmut.

I wish Ryan was here... -X-

I WISH I COULD SNOG PATRICK SWAYZE

I wish my sister would flippin' well tidy up her mess!

LONDON W1F 7JE
LEON.
35-36 Gt. MARLBOROUGH St.
Fair Trade & Organic
NOME DEL
PASSEGGERO _____
BAGAGLIAIO

FRESH FISH
from
sustainable shoals

DOLPHIN
FRIENDLY

THE LEON GOBI
1 2 3 4 5 6 7 8 9 10 11 12 S

SUPERFOOD SALAD
LEON ORIGINAL

LEON-HOTEL
CASABLANCA

LEON
35 GREAT MARLBOROUGH STREET   LONDON   W1F 7JE   T: 020 7437 5280

LEON
Full of Sun
35 GT. MARLBOROUGH ST.
LONDON

LEON
OUR FISH IS FROM SUSTAINABLE SHOALS OR FARMED ORGANICALLY

LEON   LDN.

I wish to fall in love!
I WISH I WAS A POLAR BEAR
I WISH MY GRANDMA WAS HERE.
I wish I was sane
I WISH I WAS WRITING THE MOST BEAUTIFUL BOOK EVER UPON AN ITALIAN TERRACE WITH AN ENDLESS SUPPLY OF PASTA, CHAMPAGNE AND SUNDRESSES
I WISH MY JOB DIDN'T SUCK.
I wish Greg would move to London.
I wish I know what this drawer was for

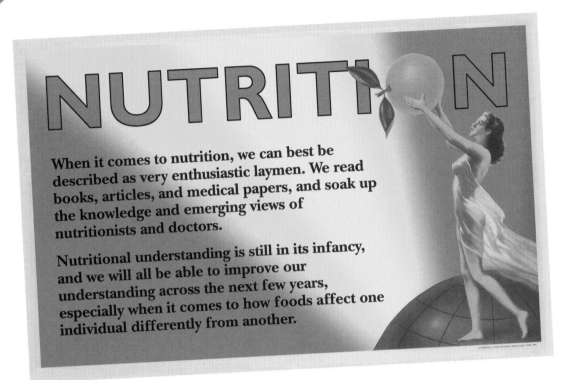

NUTRITION

When it comes to nutrition, we can best be described as very enthusiastic laymen. We read books, articles, and medical papers, and soak up the knowledge and emerging views of nutritionists and doctors.

Nutritional understanding is still in its infancy, and we will all be able to improve our understanding across the next few years, especially when it comes to how foods affect one individual differently from another.

Here, we'd like to explain the significance behind the icons we use and how these principles might be useful to you as you shop and eat more generally.

✓ We use the ✓ symbol to denote dishes that have a low "Glycemic Load" or GL. This is a concept that has become much better understood in the past five years. It is slightly different from the more famous Glycemic Index (GI), which measures the sugariness of the carbohydrate within each food, on a scale relative to glucose (which ranks at 100). On the GI all foods with a score above 50 are seen as bad news, even though some—a carrot, say— might contain only a small amount of the offending carbohydrate.

The Glycemic Load, by contrast, measures the effect of the whole food (i.e. the whole carrot), not just the sugary element. This means that carrots, which score badly on the Glycemic Index, score well on GL because they contain very little carbohydrate. What matters—in terms of keeping you healthy—is the extent to which a food raises your blood sugar levels as it is digested, promoting the buildup of fat. We give any dish with a GL of under 10 a ✓.

 These dishes have less than 1.5 percent saturated fat. Most people need to eat more oily fats, such as olive oil, fishy fats, the fats found in vegetables, such as avocado, in seeds, and nuts, and even goose fat. These are now recognized as essential to health and even weightloss. (There are a very few people who actually need to eat more hard, saturated fats.) None of our food has modified fats, such as trans fats.

W F   For a number of reasons, wheat has become a problem for many people. Modern wheat is very different from traditional "old" grains, such as buckwheat, millet, spelt, and kamut. Over the centuries, it has been bred to be easier to harvest and higher yielding. Along the way, the average gluten content of wheat has soared from 2 percent to 50 percent, perhaps accounting for the increase in wheat intolerance. There is also evidence that the protein in wheat germ is causing health issues for many people.

D F   All mammals, including man, need milk in infancy. But as adults, many of us lose the enzymes needed to digest milk and other dairy products, leading to digestive problems. Thus the DF icon.

G F   Celiac disease is the most extreme manifestation of gluten intolerance. But research suggests that all of us would be healthier if we cut down on gluten—the protein that gives many starches their stickiness. It exists in wheat, rye, barley, and other related grains—but not in any of these dishes.

V   Vegetarian. Because we should all be eating more veg.

   Indulgence. We believe in letting our hair down occasionally. These dishes—to be enjoyed on special occasions—will invigorate the spirit.

So what general advice can one give? Most of us thrive best on moderate portions of naturally produced food, predominantly vegetables, with plenty of the foods that we used to scavenge for: seeds, berries, nuts. And with side helpings of meat. As Michael Pollan says in his excellent *In Defense of Food*: "Eat food. Not too much. Mostly plants."

We've spoken to a lot of people along the way to deepen our understanding of nutrition, and among those who we'd like to thank are Yvonne Bishop-Weston and Carole Symons, who have been particularly helpful.

Henry and Liza, southern Spain, August 1977

INDEX

INDEX

INDEX

INDEX

INDEX

Charlie Bigham • Nicola Williams • Guy McLaren • Helen Vaughan • Helen Cruise • Laura Schofield • Jamie Gorman • Monica Peswani • Lloyd Hughes • Tom Bell • Mark Latham • Kenny McColl • Martin Bull • Russell Loveland • David Atcherley-Symes • Camille Waxer • Henry Togna • Paul Wakefield • Ben Kilshaw • Nigel Mason • Andy Maunder • Craig & Clare Barton • Clare Mugglestone • Carly Stevenson • Birgit Gunz • Emma & Matt Goss-Custard • Simon Pritchard • Derek Aston • Guy Lingard • Gary Ashcroft • Kevin Hayler • Nick Wood • Caroline Babington • Monica Wolff • David Kaye • Martin Sansom • Mary Purnell • Alex Maynard

Skye Gygnell for inspiring a whole new breed of Leon wrap

Nick Stratton for showing people how great a human being can be

Sandra whose initial Leon designs live on

Thank you to Katie "the wife" Derham for constant sunshine, encouragement and ideas

To all of you who have eaten with us & allowed us to realize the first steps of our dreams

JoJo for her gardening wisdom

Bambi Sloane for riding the roller coaster and still managing to design while on it —you channel the spirit of a thousand artists

Fred for his infectious enthusiasm

Jane at the Riverford Farm Field Kitchen for helping me see vegetables in a new light

Richard Reed for being my life-twin and for the foot thing (although I can never be Sifu Sifu Jones)

Vivian Imerman for being the Godfather

Simon, Benny, James, Tom, Rich, Agnieszka, and Steve for keeping the Leon show on the road

Allegra for everything she did to get us up and running

Xander, Adam, Dave, Becca, Lloyd, James, Ian, Susana, Jonathan, Michele, & Belinda for believing in Leon from the start

Anita for doing away with sleep to get this book out of the door (almost) on time

Annie Lee for copy editing

Steph Morison for being a brilliant human being

Natasha and Eleanor for fierce loyalty. And for being brilliant, loving daughters.

Alice Denford for bringing new dimensions.

Claire for the cakes

Mattma, Maddie and Cy for props, love & patience

David Griffiths for advertently and inadvertently giving me everything I have had since the age of 19

Cameron, Isla, Shickadee, George & Ned for gurning.

Andy & Glenys for testing and testing and testing

Marc Rogers • Sophie Douglas • Roger Gascoigne • Rick Hudson • Tony Bamford-Mumby • Jack Sharkey • Chris Rouine • Adrian Eade • Andy Oldham • Vic Madhu • Simon Watkins • Anne Philippe • Leticia Godet • Peter Wakeling • Fabio Di Palma • Dan Taylor • Yvette Doughty • Nick Wesley • Abigail Lawley • Jethro McCarthy • Jon Horsfield • Cara Coan • Alecia Mitchell • Ian Carpenter • Rod Adlington • James Fincham • The Big Chill tent construction gang • Andy Kellar • Gemma Alashe

THANK YOU

Jo, Nicky, Laura, Amy and Danni at Sauce • Polly Brunt (for lots of things but also for being there when I sent that Carnaby email) • Paul Burke for copy inspiration (inc "it won't help you rule the world. It's much better than that") • Trevor Shelley who believed in us and supported us right from the start (rest in peace my friend) • Jonathan Moradoff for a bit of the above, too • Marc Rogers who found us Spitalfields • Ian Hunt for passion and intuition • Dino and Marcel • Andrew Matthews Owen for the macaroons and hilarity • James Horler • Carol and Nick • Angus Graham for being a best best friend and helping in so many ways at the start of Leon • Kate Quick for the last six months • Kate Hughes for your stint as FD • John Lotherington and Andy Rattue • Steve Coltrin • JP, Cath, Lauren, and Hannah (Salty's or BBQ?) • Matilda Harrison

and Sue

Georgia for stunning photos and a fabulously dirty laugh

Nita, Joe, Tim Joanne, Joseph, Charlotte, Frank, Tracey, Georgis, Imogen, Kate, Gordon, Sarah Jayne, AJ, Luke, Nick, Carys, Mischa, Lois, Theya, Migs, Will, David and Cassandra, Richard, Qing, Anne, John, Pop & Helen as clans matter

Hattie for lighting up any room she enters and for holding the whole thing together

THANK YOU

Nicole and Tony from Food Alert

To my wife Mima: for her encouragement and support; for putting up with my endless fussing about Leon; for her proof reading; for her cooking; and most of all for her extraordinary patience and understanding

FRESH FISH TODAY

Mitch Tonks for sharing his passion for fish so generously

Lorraine, Jonathan, Sybella, and everyone at Conran Octopus for believing in us a second time around

Liam Bailey, Elektra Mandy & Flora McEvedy for photographs & paintings

Apple for food inspiration & positivity

Giuslan Oliveira Andade, Giancarlo Lanzillo, Emma Greeff, Tahsin Kucuk, Frida Alderin, Magdalena Czyzowska,

Ophelia Conheady, Deividas Trainavicius, Natalia Koc, Erwan Colonneau, Francesca Fadda, Arron Leppard, Adele Flurry, Martyn Trigg, Shalayne Lindemann, Matt Lineham, Sophie Akister, Rochelle Louise McGarrity, Jirina Kralova, Manca Dezman, Christine Noel, Katre Kurosu, Yok Ming Chung, Simon Ruseell, Kristaps Sorins, Alejandro Medina Leos, , Santona Alam, Radoslaw Zemsta, Jacek Swiatkowski, Karin Hagg, Matteo Di Cugno, Robert Beaney, Gary Marriott, Josh Lawrence, Leighanne Diarcy, Alexandra Ellison, Liberty Antrobus, Chiok-Sing Li, Alexandria Caplin, Stacey Marshall, Marques Christian, Jasmin Sangha, Marc Rogers, Giancarlo Lanzillo,

Anita for her beautiful designs and refusal to be phased as deadlines hurtled toward her

Bobby Dhadwal, Simon Teale, Stacie Johnson, Holly Clare, Ciara Costigan, Jack Wythe, Nikki Munro, Gemma Jones, Wendy Cooper, Ashleigh Davewport, Joanna Puddle, Scott Humphrey, Aisha Tohme, Kayliegh Hook, Matthew Ali, Malgorzata Glazowska, Stephane Guillaumet, Laura Silova, Jessyca Manfredini, David Green, Jenny Mainusch, Diletta Tanzini, Jin Qian, Hui Wen Law, Karolina Jurga, Martyn Trigg, Juraj Jurovcik, Lara Wrubel, Jenna Brehme, Therese Noren, Shipon Miah, Szilard Zsovak, Jose Antonio Montano Gaviria, Cirican Vasilica Romana, Hillary Tabah, Rodrigo Borrero, Mercedes Duch, Claudemir Esteuam de Nogueira, Peter Gartside, Amie Hooper, Joanna Wyrwicz, Houtan Obadai, Asuncion Valero, Jose Ricardo Zim Nunez, Heber Oliveira, Malin Scanavino,

Miranda, Jo, Pierre, and Jon

Dougie & Claudia Douglas • Kevin Lidlow, Gowrin Motha, Chris Enser • Dominic Wilhelm

Wellness gurus Wendy Mandy, Wendle Nightingale, Mounir Tourabi, Carole Symons,

Malgorzata Charmaine Sylvia Lowe, Lee Hay, Gemma Louise Hunt, Patche Mendy, Mateosz Warpas, Hannah Jarvis Howard, Roswita Taylor, Olivier Le Mire, Fabio Constabile, Janet Taylor, Sebastian Nemcek, Denise Vilela, Siaro Isse, Wioletta Woloszyn, Simon Drysdale, Thomas Ward, Louis Mourlan, Pam Leung, Cedric Montella, Hedi Putallaz, Claudia Barbarotto, Ewa Socha, Lukasz Milak, Piers Harrisson, Floriane Miletic, Diego Oliveira, Chloe Hignett, Agata Szczerecka, Michaela Smazakova, Vikas Kumar, Joe Lynam, Marielle Anguis, Marine Guichard, Javier Lavin, Mubina Fattoum, Ramone Stewart, Chloe Taylor, Nina Kaczkowska, Carlos Gonzales, Efemena Okogba1, Daniella Guimaraes, Johanna Rooth, Claire O`Keeffe, Gabriela Nicola, Zeyana Al-Mahrizy, Asher Michael Dresner, Magdalena Myskow, Ingrid Chopard-Lallier, Davi Borges, Carolina Sierra Romero, Andre Putzier, Egle Narbutaite, Gerda Viljastu, Dilan Kotan, Candy Alderson, Natallia Paulava, Wioletta Jamrozek, Polly Brunt, Edivanio Ferreira, Julia Karimzanova, Simon Joe Portal, Zhuola Lu, James McCormack, Sebastian Grebos, Piia Vilja, Kaori Tsuchiida, Karina Reyes, Kate Middlemiss, Marta Karcz, Juliana Martins Silva, Viktor Lenken, Lawrence Bowen, Cristina Castro, Mazarra Mazerati, Audrey Colonna, Inah Lee, Mayo Cimarra, Celine Weber, Nishantha Pallawatta, Juraj Mastihuba, Ivana Bednarova, Anna Kalinska, Stephanie Garcia-Brazzalotto, Laila Vaziralli, Remigijus Chmieliauskas, Maria Okanrende, Evelyn Ferek, Justyna Rezler, Melody Grelat, Marcos Garrido, Chiara Scipioni, Persia Aitken-Edwards, Cristian Causa Cecere, Laurence Breva, Otoa Ise, Claudio Ramin, Maria Zywicka, Yunus Khaydarov, Fabiano Texeira, Crispim Jose Dos Santos, Anna Freijlich, Shirley Cussi, Maurycy Maciejewicz, Justyna Konca, Erika Kubesova, Yumi Kaneko, John Peter Vespa, Anna Sobczak, Florent Genon-Catalot, Tameira McLean, Hannah Jean La Palombara, Theodore Lestrade, Zuzana Krojidlova, Orlan Masilu-Lokubike, Jon Lopez, Dominik Poczekala, Marta Majewska, Jean-Noel Hardelin, Teja Hudson, Mohamed Ait Ahmed Ouali, Dorota Barczynska, Joost Pronk, Agnes Czolnowska, Maciej Marek, Catherine Elizabet Neeson, John Cole, Wairimu Mburathi, Piotr Jablonski, Jurga Stackeviciute, Cesar Sandrin, Pedro Francisque,Mariusz Janicki, Charlotte Olsson, Vagner Bustamante, Malgorzata Smiejkowska, Kamila Kurasinska, Piotr Glabicki, Carlos Rabanillo, Gregory Rosamont, Vanessa Jarrin, Mayuko Sugimitsu, Nicola Sutcliffe, Anna Marczenko, David Smit, Isabel Merino, Kevin Gendron, Rodrigo Luis Ferreira, Piotr Slabonski, Stanley John Hornsey, Krystian Wilegosz, Marcin Dawicki, Krzysztof Borkowski, Jolita Cekaviciute, Anne-Charlotte Lataste, Joanna Klimczak, Queralt Torrent Llamas, Remy Orciac, Arran O`Neill, Marcio Gonzales Silva, Giovanni Luca Cucurachi, Edyta Plawecka, Stephen Oakley, Maciej Zuchowski, Sini Marika Mulari, Jenny Lundqvist, Christina Binder, Amanda Silva, Almir Godinho, Andreas Friedrich, Elsa Bonafonte, Alexander Lejava, Nivia Marshall, Marisol Cardenas Gallo, Anais Lasselin, Marcin Rozanski, Simon Wilbers, Caitlin McMullin, Marzena Zielinska, Janina Shabel, Kadija Begum, Eduardo Petry, Sandra Petrasevic, Lesley Strafford, Leila Vaziralli, Michal Wowalkowski, Haoyi Wang, Afonso Padras, Efemena Okogba, Daniele Massino Ciprian, Imogen Hamilton, Jorg Jauernig, Cesar Guerrero, Marina Falabella, Kazimierz Mazur, Ellie Richold, Peter Ternai, Dariusz Lamecki, Fabio Rodrigues, Sagarvarum Sharma, Tereza Sera, Sandra Cieslak, Sarah Lever, Samuel Sallah, David Sandoval Garcia, Robert Malicin, Miguel Torres, David Febrero lopez, Tero Saavalainen, Daniele Meus, Henry Hryn Acosta, Nathalia Franco, Alicja Merska, Agata Cyminska, Edward Bocanegra, Pedro Carvalho, Cerys Bowen, Dimitar Ralev, Karolina Jurga, Mitchell Kardon, Tomasz Kolakowski, Dauron Boltaev, Bing Xia, Lorena Ponte, Laura Power, Laure Darcel, Miriam Gontijo, Jose Luis Merino Garcia, Adulai Sabali, Fiona Tang, Tita Cvetkovic, Robert Doka, Cong Fu, Alex Thirlwell, Karolina Stepien, Kerry Turley, Mario Rusponi, Marek Micek, Oyeniran Babatunde, Reyes Romero, Ryan Finnegan, Marija Burdulyte, Alisson Grossi, Denis Tomka, Anna-Cecile Laboure, Andrew Hunt, Guillaume Burguez, Morgen Lorandel, Leonardo Gueli, Brandon Hillman, Miguel Fontalvo, Emoke Kilin, Pietro Verde, Tameira McLean, Muge Pancar, Judit Andrassy, Emily Hermon, Manuela Blahova, Ricardo Ditz, Xiaoguang Xu, Alba Vidal, Bruno Massaccesi, Pedro Miguel Camargo Da Cunha Rego, Ann Jorgensen, Hector Palacios, Jose Antonio Moreno, Aneta Jurkowlaniec, Julia Karimzanova, Kassandra Kay, Lindsay Taylor, Stefanos Gkouts, Agnieszka Sobolewska,Muhammad Rizwan Shahid, Joao Trindade, Fernando Roberto Santo, Christiane Silva, Bethany Ward, Gavin Williams, Jefferson Freitas, Christian Javier Caguana Telenchana, Jay Bernard, Kimberly Morris, Fatou Gaye, Emilie Fournet, Combes Guillaume, Rodrigo Menezes De Carvalho, Jana Pajtasova, Inta Lankovska, Ilona Palij, Kirsten Fonzari, Cedric Havard, Nabil Bourassi, Kher Ying Tey, Joanna Czwakiel, Asad Khan, Sabine Agoston, Greg Russell, Kristal Maley, Lysette Cook, Kashaka Marcano, Tom Green, Lucy Buckingham, Matthew Alp, Igor Kurosu, May Kovacova, Joe Lawrence, Claire Tully, Rute Christina Coelho da Rocha, Chloe Martin, Deivid Grigorid, Marta Kowalska, Chiara Scipioni, Jason Ferreira, Rachel Little, Eric Goncalves, Giuliano Giannini, Mariana Gontijo, Edward Bocanegra, Attiya Batool, Paulina Konieczka-Jurkiewicz, Ruth Saunders, Gabor Marton, John O`Sullivan, Ella Baruch, Luis De Pablo Olivenza, Alice Watson, Olivia Lewis, Ulpu Inkeri Korhonen, Bozena Bobowska, Fernanda Bondioli, Liliya Georgieva, S.M Ruhul Amin, Lory Clement, Samy Dion, Hannah Newman, Loreesa Timms, Marta Dabrowka, Carolina Jilderson Svensson, Sebastien Munch, Sylvain Francescato, Corvin Dhali, Daniel Scott, Fabricio Feliciano, Giedre Pociute, Bjorn Tirsen, Jacqueline Tong, Louise Mochia, Ben Rider, Jessica Huguet, Marina Murinova, Lenka Hajnovicova, Vjaceslavs Sadovskis, Rafa Gesla, Lauren Nightingale, Weronika Wlostowska, Natalia Zajaczkowska, Lennie Coindeaux, Karolina Ciulemba, Elizabeth Okogba, Queralt Torrent Llamas, Danilo Santos, Rodrigo Muniz, Bhovinder Singh, Izabela Zeliszczak, Luna Turner, Peter Chytil, Diana Nikolic, Kyle Bellamy, Sarah Young, Tiago Michaelson, Izabela Antosiewicz, Jessica Dornieden, Bruno Lupi, Marta Adamczyk, Tameira McLean, Jackson Freitas, Thiago Cuadra Garcia, Phoebe Mayer, Filip Tedelund, Anderson Da Silva, Andres Mendoza, Richard Holmes, Laura Davey, Juliana Rodrigues Mourlan, Rogerio Rius Balestrin, Kassem Yassin, Malgorzata Smiejkowska, Karina Reyes, Leoniel Morson, Ben Iredale, Andre Teixeira, Jozef Depta, Anja Otto, Elizeu De Moura, Suzanne Carter, Danilo Cacciola, Marek Micek, Danielius Jancauskas, Robson Ribeiro, Roberta Borovskis, Ljojcields Hylko, Paulo Rodrigues, Joanna Herbert, Aroa Ruiz, Luiz Fernando De Custodio, Isabela Santos, B Tunde, Sandra Svobodova, Yi Chen Sun, Marco Angelino, Dayane Piffer, Ruby Eyre, Melek Halil, Marius Lakatos, Rodrigues Cleverson Antonio, Francesco Rossello, Federica Porcu, Lucyjana Gomes de Sousa, Kudratjon Fattakhov, Marek Micek, Ben Iredale, Lane Gabitass, Daniel Martinez Molero, Sun Liang, Thibaut Strappazon, Wojciech Szczepaniak, Zybowski Jaroslaw, Candy Alderson, Lea Skender, Caroline Linhares, Eleanor Robertson, Bibek Singh, Luiz Alberto Mende De Oliveira, Barry Neale, Rogerio Rius Balestrin, Ronaldo Alves, Carolina Pereira, Yago Abella, Luiz Oliveira, Efemena Okogba, Bernardo Novaes, Lucas Darienco Valenca, Malgorzata Krogulec, Claudia Cocci Gifroni, Laura Pares, Lina Soderland, Tahsin Kucuk, Joanna Marek, Piotr Maciej Michalski, Renato Fernandes, Karolina Jurga, Emma Lejonqvist, Golam Shohan, Elwira Miechowiecka, Maciej Popiolek, Luisa Cruz, Myintzu Zeyya, Linda Abdelhak, Ewa Szawurska, Lisa McCarthy, Masako Miyazaki, Fedrica Scuito, Wilson Fernandes, Orlan Masilu, Martina Merickova, Jenny Russell, Renan Amorin, Nicolas Bracamonte, Mara Casolari, Ingrida Jurovcikova, Queraat Torrent llamas, Antonio Cardoso, Natalia Balbi Amato, Sofia Leddin, Pavel Novacek, Roberta Rimkute, Martha Doria, Elisa Santacatterina, Onur Eminogloa, Pedro Ribeiro, Wesley Alves, Vinicius Da Silva,Anthonia Ijegwa Adaji, Rikki William Payne, Christopher Swinbourne, Lee Jason Concannon, Jamie Brenchley, Stephen Bage, Lauren Griffin, Charlotte Thompson, Cheyne Mcmillian, Gemma Lim, Daniel Britton, Sophia Hodson, Lucy Harrison,

Matthew Gordon for being generosity and for being very cool (focus)• Wally Olins, mentor and friend • Spencer, Nick and Gavyn at Active • Roger Siddle for accepting me into the cult • Nick Jackson for keeping me there • Michele Luzi, Mark Gwynne, and Lloyd – may your reward be on earth • We remember Caroline, Brahim, and Jay And finally Lenny Kogan (you know who you aren't)

Adam, Sophie, Clemmy, Daisy, and Nat Blaker for Sussex love • Kenny and Gabby Logan for friendship (although I don't like the painting with the small heads) • Paul Hayler for early encouragement Mr. Hart and Mrs. Clarke for very early encouragement

Giles and Mark for conceiving the Sustainable Restaurant Association and asking me along for the ride

To my Mom & Dad for magically combining support, warmth, counsel, and just as importantly, fun and adventure

Roly and Susan neighborly support

Bruno Loubet for giving me my first job and encouraging me to follow a career in food

Henry, for being a brilliant business partner

All the ladies in the Bluewater job shop for all their help when we opened • Gemma H.
Len Green (Ludgate) • Yenny • Stephen from Learn Purple • Gemma H.
• Dave & John from Emtone printing • Jo Fontaine from Fishbowl
Iona McDonald from Addison Fowle • Kris Anderson
Bluewater Management Team
Yvette from Tibard
Jason Cooper

Dedications:
For my Mother and Father. — HD
For my Mom and Dad. Thank you for so much. And Katie, Natasha, and Eleanor. Thank you for everything else. — JV

First published in UK in 2010 by Conran Octopus Limited, a part of Octopus Publishing Group,
Endeavour House, 189 Shaftesbury Avenue, London WC2H 8JY
An Hachette UK Company www.hachette.co.uk

First published in US in 2012, distributed by Hachette Book Group USA, 237 Park Avenue, New York NY 10017 USA

Distributed in Canada by Canadian Manda Group, 165 Dufferin Street, Toronto, Ontario, Canada M6K 3H6

British Library Cataloguing-in-Publication Data.
A catalogue record for this book is available from the British Library.

Publisher: Lorraine Dickey
Managing Editor: Sybella Marlow
Project Manager & Co-cooker: Hattie Deards

Art Director (for Leon): Anita Mangan
Art Director (for Conran Octopus): Jonathan Christie
Illustrations: Anita Mangan (except pages 14–15 Elektra Mandy; 176–77, 202–3 Flora McEvedy; 165 Madelaine Cooper)
Special Photography: Georgia Glynn Smith

Production Manager: Katherine Hockley

Anita and Stephen, 1970

Every effort has been made to trace the images' copyright holders, and we
apologize in advance for any unintentional omissions, and would be pleased
to insert the appropriate acknowledgement in any subsequent publication.

ISBN: 978 1 84091 612 6
Printed in China